JUDY GERRY

FACING ADVERSITY

Transforming the Storms of Life Into Seasons of Blessing

SOMIS, CALIFORNIA 93066

ISBN: 978-0-9799116-1-3
Copyright 2009 by LifeSong Publishers

Published by LifeSong Publishers
P.O. Box 183, Somis, CA 93066-0183
805-504-3916
www.lifesongpublishers.com

All rights reserved. Reproduction or use of the editorial or pictorial content of this material in any manner is prohibited by law without the express permission from the publisher.

Unless otherwise noted, all Bible quotations are from the New American Standard Bible.

Scripture taken from the NEW AMERICAN STANDARD BIBLE. Copyright 1960, 1962, 1963, 1968, 1971, 1972, 1973, 1975, 1977, 1995 by the Lockman Foundation. Used by permission.

Scripture taken from the HOLY BIBLE, NEW INTERNATIONAL VERSION®. Copyright © 1973, 1978, 1984 International Bible Society. Used by permission of Zondervan. All rights reserved.

Scripture taken from the New King James Version. Copyright © 1982 by Thomas Nelson, Inc. Used by permission. All rights reserved.

Library of Congress Cataloging-in-Publication Data

Gerry, Judy.
  Facing adversity : transforming the storms of life into seasons of blessing / by Judy Gerry.
  p. cm.

  Includes bibliographical references.
  ISBN 978-0-9799116-1-3 (pbk.)
  1. Suffering--Religious aspects--Christianity. I. Title.
  BV4909.G47 2009
  248.8'6--dc22
                        2008053878

Endorsements

Judy Gerry is a wise, compassionate woman of God. This study will lead you to a deeper understanding of God's perspective on pain and His loving purposes in adversity. It will enable you to go beyond coping with trials, to rejoicing in them and allowing them to produce rich results in your life.

--Nancy Leigh DeMoss, Author, Revive Our Hearts radio host

"Can there be anything good about bad times? In her excellent study, 'Facing Adversity," Judy Gerry takes her readers on a scriptural pilgrimage in search of an answer to this often-raised question. Benefited by the author's refreshing clarity, solid faith and spiritual insight, the reader will discover that the answer is a resounding 'Yes!' Adversity, in fact, is portrayed as an essential element on every Christians path toward spiritual maturity. Judy Gerry shows the pilgrim how to embrace hard times with the grace of God."

--Tom Elliff, Senior Pastor, Missionary, Author
Past President, Southern Baptist Convention

Adversity is a normal part of life. It tests the metal from which we are made. Yet, God often gives great grace and wisdom through our trials if we see them through the lenses of His eyes. God has a way of making adversity our best friend.

...Judy Gerry leads us to the Scriptures to discover victory in the midst of adversity. She teaches us to see trials, problems and sorrows from a Biblical perspective. She leads us to waters that turn bitter circumstances into bountiful blessings and difficult days into Divine deliverance. She brings us to the Word of God and encourages us to look at adversity through His eyes.

You will be blessed by Judy's insights. I highly encourage you to read, study, and pray through the message encapsulated in this book. When the storms of life come, you will find yourself standing in a place of safety and victory as you understand and apply these great truths to your life.

--Sammy Tippit, Sammy Tippit Ministries

ACKNOWLEDGEMENTS

I acknowledge that my natural inclination is to resist and resent all adversity. But I praise God that His ways and thoughts are better than mine (Isaiah 55:9). He has used stormy trials in my life to propel me into places of blessing that I would never have known otherwise.

This Bible study is the cumulative result of God's divine intervention in my own life, and in the lives of His children, over generations.

- Thank you, Father, for parents who nudged me into Your arms during my childhood (Deuteronomy 4:9).

- Thank You, Lord, for my husband Dave who has victoriously walked with me through many of life's dark valleys (Song of Solomon 5:16; Ecclesiastes 4:12).

- Thank You, God of all Comfort, for family and friends who have shared with me their personal life struggles. Their lives have steadfastly encouraged and exhorted me to persevere during my own trials (II Corinthians 1:3).

- Thank You, Jesus, for Your Holy Word which teaches me how to see my circumstances from Your perspective and cooperate with Your plan for my life (II Timothy 3:16, 17).

- Thank You, Prince of Peace, for the Holy Spirit who exuberantly compels my heart to rejoice in my sufferings (I Peter 1:6, 7).

- Thank You, for the "unseen cloud of witnesses" who cheer me on daily (Hebrews 12:1).

- Thank You, Sovereign God, for Your servant Laurie Donahue whose vision and generosity have made this material widely available to others (Psalm 26:7).

- Thank You, Father, for the graciousness of Your children who have humbly helped with this study; Nancy Leigh DeMoss, Dr. Tom Elliff, Sammy Tippit, and others who have edited and endorsed this material with the singular goal to serve Your people (Hebrews 6:10).

- And Thank You, Lord, that You are preparing us to meet You soon. May this study be an impetus for Your children to "face adversity" with victory and joy. I pray that.....

the Spirit of God will use
the Word of God to make
the Child of God like
the Son of God
....until we see You face to face (I John 3:2).

Maranatha!

Judy

Contents

Preface — 7

Week 1: *The Problem With Pain* — 9

Week 2: *Putting Adversity into Perspective* — 23

Week 3: *The Positive Side of Negative* — 39

Week 4: *Adversity Enables Us to See Ourselves* — 55

Week 5: *Adversity Teaches Us to Depend on God* — 73

Week 6: *Adversity Clarifies our Purpose in Life* — 89

Week 7: *Adversity Prepares Us for Blessing* — 101

Week 8: *Adversity Is an Invitation from God* — 115

Bibliography — 131

Facing Adversity

PREFACE

Adversity is a painful fact of life. Everyone experiences set-backs, disappointment, trials, and grief. Contemporary society proposes a myriad of suggestions regarding how to deal with such hurts. Advice commentators abound.

Yet God's Word provides the only accurate perspective on pain and Scripture reveals great insight into how to respond to affliction. God's ways are not our ways (Isaiah 55:8), and He uses everything in our lives to accomplish His purposes (Romans 8:28).

The wise believer seeks to cooperate with the Lord during the storms of life. When we are pliable in His hands, we can watch the turbulent times of life become transformed into seasons of great blessing.

This Bible study is intended to take the student directly into God's Word in order to gain a perspective on adversity. If we can catch a vision of God's purposes for pain and learn to respond to trials in a biblical way, then we can cooperate with the Lord as He accomplishes His unique purposes for our lives. We will become prepared for ministry, future blessing will be ensured, and the Lord Jesus will be glorified.

Rather than learning to merely "cope" with life during the hard times, God's Word tells us how we can be victorious "overcomers."

> *"These things I have spoken to you, that in Me you may have peace.*
> *In the world you have tribulation, but take courage;*
> *I have overcome the world." (John 16:33)*

Rather than sensing a diminished relationship with the Lord during turbulent times, God's Word tells us that He is waiting to meet us intimately as we cry out for Him in the storm. It is actually in the thunder that God is hiding.

> *"You called in trouble and I rescued you;*
> *I answered you in the hiding place of thunder." (Psalm 81:7a)*

It took me many years as a Christian to recognize that the Lord was using trials to induce my spiritual growth. Rather than viewing the storms of life as something to bitterly endure, God's Word tells us that whirlwinds may actually carry us to higher realms of victory and blessing.

It is my prayer that through this study you will learn practical truths that will help you turn "set-backs into stepping-stones" and "adversity into advantage." Every sorrow that we experience is an opportunity for spiritual growth. Once we get a glimpse of how the Lord uses our trials to accomplish glorious results, it really IS possible to quickly and eagerly rejoice when FACING ADVERSITY!

WEEK 1

The Problem With Pain

DAY 1: DEALING WITH THE INITIAL SHOCK

Life is a gift from God intended to be savored and enjoyed. It is easy to be thankful and joyful when life is a series of pleasant "Kodak moments." No one on earth, however, is exempt from the reality of pain. Life's first introduction to the world is itself accomplished through the painful process of childbirth.

While most adversity is temporary, there are turbulent times of hardship which challenge our understanding of life. There are seasons when the darkening clouds of trouble seem to gather all around us. While desperately hoping that problems will dissipate in the breeze, they gain intensity. The winds begin to howl, the thunder threatens and the whirlwind rages on. We wonder what on earth is happening.

During these storms of adversity, we cry out for God to deliver us. Everything in us longs to escape:

> "My heart is in anguish within me, and the terrors of death have fallen upon me. Fear and trembling come upon me; and horror has overwhelmed me. And I said, 'Oh, that I had wings like a dove! I would fly away and be at rest. Behold, I would wander far away, I would lodge in the wilderness. Selah.
> I would hasten to my place of refuge from the stormy wind and tempest.'"
> *(Psalm 55:4-8)*

Facing Adversity

Adversity is by definition painful. It is "a condition of suffering, destitution, or affliction; a calamitous or disastrous experience." (Webster)

Synonyms for adversity include: *hard times, rainy day, gathering clouds, ill-wind, affliction, trouble, hardship, curse, blight, load, pressure, mishap, disaster, calamity, trial, sorrow, setback, chastening, anguish, opposition, testing, and tribulation.*

Would you say that you ever experienced adversity? Describe the situation:

What was your initial reaction to the situation? What thoughts went through your mind? How did you feel?

The initial shock that we feel when we encounter trials usually results in several reactions. We often think that the situation is unbelievable, unbearable, totally out-of-the-ordinary, or unfair. The Lord speaks to each of these reactions in His Word. Look up the following verses and record your insights. Note any reaction that you have experienced.

   "This is unbelievable! Things like this aren't supposed to happen."

    1.   Job 5:7

    2.   John 16:33

    3.   I Thessalonians 3:3, 4

Week 1: The Problem with Pain

4.　　Job 2:10

"I can't bear this! It is too much for me to handle."

5.　　Hebrews 4:15, 16

6.　　Philippians 4:13

"Why me? Other people don't experience things like this!"

7.　　I Peter 4:12

8.　　I Corinthians 10:13

"This is not fair! There is no justice in life!"

9.　　Luke 18:1-8

10.　　II Corinthians 5:10

11.　　Revelation 20:11-13

12.　　I Peter 2:19-21

Facing Adversity

"Lord, this situation that I'm facing is painful; I'm confused right now. I need You to help me to understand what is going on, and how I should respond to what is happening. You've promised that You will always be with me and that You will strengthen me. So I cry out to You today, asking You help me. I can't see what is going on around me, but I trust You, Father. Amen."

The Problem With Pain
DAY 2: WHAT'S GOING ON?

There is a lot of erroneous teaching regarding suffering today, even in the church. We need to evaluate what we believe in the light of God's Word. Note any theory below that you have heard, then look up the Scripture references for insight to determine what is true.

 Adversity only happens to bad people. Spiritual people don't have trouble.

1. II Timothy 3:12

2. Job 1:1

3. John 19:6

4. Psalm 34:19

Week 1: The Problem with Pain

 We're never to ask for adversity to be removed.

    5.   Luke 22:42

    6.   Job 13:15, 16

 God does not want us to know why painful things happen.

    7.   II Corinthians 12:7

 Suffering is an illusion; pain is not real.

    8.   John 20:27

THE TRUTH IS THAT ADVERSITY IS REAL. IT IS PAINFUL. AND IT HAPPENS TO EVERYONE.

"Father, I don't like being in pain. I would rather not have to go through this difficult time. But, like Jesus, the thing that I want the most is to experience Your will for my life. Lord, please help me to control my thoughts and emotions so that I can see what is really true. Thank You for understanding how I feel, and for encouraging me with Your presence. I trust You, Lord. Amen."

Facing Adversity

The Problem With Pain

DAY 3: WHERE DID THIS COME FROM?

The first reaction of one who is suffering is to stop the pain. Perhaps if one could discern the origin of the affliction it might facilitate ending the agony.

"Where does adversity come from? If God is in control, why would He allow such troubles to enter my life?" These questions and others occur to the one enduring the sorrow of suffering. While God has not always promised us answers, He has promised to always be with us and to continually love us.

The Lord lovingly points out to us in Scripture that there are three basic sources of adversity.

A. ADVERSITY CAN BE THE BY-PRODUCT OF PERSONAL SIN:

Early in human history, Adam and Eve experienced life-altering adversity when they chose to sin (Genesis 3:16-19). Today our personal sin continues to lead to our personal pain. Note what the following verses say about sin.

    1.   James 1:14, 15

    2.   Romans 2:9

    3.   Job 4:8

    4.   Jeremiah 5:25

Week 1: The Problem with Pain

    5.   Galatians 6:7, 8

God speaks of the "Law of the Harvest" in His Word:

       We will reap WHAT we sow,
       We will reap MORE than we sow,
       We will reap LATER than we sow.

Can you think of a time when you suffered as the result of personal sin in your own life? Describe that situation.

How could that sorrow have been avoided?

If our adversity is a result of sin, we need to assume responsibility for our own pain and confess our sin and repent. We should realize that we are reaping what we have sown and stop complaining about our hurt. With an *attitude of gratitude*, we need to thank God for loving us so much that He will not allow us to continue on with destructive sin.

B.   ADVERSITY CAN ORIGINATE WITH SATAN:

What do the following verses say about Satan's involvement with us?

    6.   I Peter 5:8, 9

Facing Adversity

7. Ephesians 6:10-12

8. Job 2:6, 7

Often the child of God is unaware that he is in the midst of a spiritual battle, and is oblivious to the fact that Satan is at the root of the troubles. Yet, the Scriptures reveal that there are certain signs (attitudes, actions, and circumstances) which may indicate an attack by Satan.

There are certain "fingerprints" of the evil one which show up when he is involved. What do you discern from the following verses to be clues that we are in direct spiritual warfare with the enemy? What are some of Satan's "fingerprints?"

9. James 3:14-16

    By contrast, what are God's "fingerprints" in I Corinthians 14:33; Isaiah 1:18?

10. Revelation 12:10 (What does Satan do to us?)

    By contrast, what are God's "fingerprints" in I John 1:9?

11. John 8:44

    By contrast, what are God's "fingerprints?" in John 14:6?

Week 1: The Problem with Pain

12.   II Timothy 1:7 (implied)

(The Greek term for "timidity" means, "a bad sense of fear and cowardice.")

13.   John 17:20-22 (implied)

Has there ever been a time when you discerned that Satan was at the root of the adversity you were experiencing?

Describe that situation, and what you did about it.

Tomorrow we will look at the third place that adversity can originate.

"Jesus, You are the light of the world. Shine Your light on my life today so that I can see what is true. Am I suffering right now because I have sinned in some way? If so, show me, Lord, and I will repent. I don't want anything coming between us, Father. Is this trial that I'm facing a direct attack from the evil one? Lord, enlighten the eyes of my heart and show me what is true. Speak to me; I am listening. Amen."

Facing Adversity

The Problem With Pain

DAY 4: WHERE IS GOD IN THIS?

"God permits what He hates...to achieve what He loves."
(Joni Eareckson Tada)

C. ADVERSITY CAN ORIGINATE WITH GOD:

It may surprise many Christians to learn that trials and adversity may actually come from God Himself. The Lord tells us in Isaiah 45:7 that He is "the One forming light and creating darkness, causing well-being and creating calamity." Note the specific types of adversity that God creates according to the verses below:

1. I Kings 11:14, 23

2. Exodus 4:11

3. Genesis 45:4-8

4. John 9:2, 3

The Lord allowed a messenger from Satan to buffet Paul (II Corinthians 12:7-10). How was God involved in the adversity that was experienced by Job?

5. Job 1:8; 2:3

Week 1: The Problem with Pain

What does the following verse imply about the existence of adversity?

6.   I Peter 3:22

Since all powers, whether evil or good, are under the control of Jesus Christ, then we can know that all things that enter our lives are there by our Lord's permission. Nothing can touch our lives without first passing through the fingers of God.

After examining our lives and being certain that our trials are NOT the result of unconfessed sin in our lives, we can know that our adversity is either from God or from Satan. Often we are unable to discern where the trial originated. Yet, regardless of its origin, we can be certain that our loving Lord is permitting it for His purposes. He does have a Divine Design.

The Lord loves to reveals much to us in His Word. Yet there are times when we cannot discern the plans that He has for allowing our affliction. God does not always reveal His plans to us.

Sometimes we cry to Him, and the heavens are silent. We look for illumination of the storm clouds, but the darkness remains. Why might the Lord withhold this information from us?

7.   Psalm 25:14

8.   Isaiah 55:8, 9

9.   Deuteronomy 29:29

When the heavens are silent, what does God want us to do?

10.   Psalm 27:13, 14

Facing Adversity

Despair results when we lose our hope that God will answer. The key to victory over despair is to wait on the Lord and take courage; believing that He has plans for our welfare (Jeremiah 29:11).

The Hebrew term "to wait" comes from a root word meaning "to twist around." Much as a bean plant entwines a pole before bearing fruit, we need to twist ourselves around Jesus and cling to Him when we're tempted to lose hope.

> *"Heavenly Father, I don't understand all that You're doing in my life, but I realize that You have allowed this trial in my life for a purpose. I believe that something good will come out of this season of difficulty. Lord, my deep desire is to wrap myself around You, and cling to You, until the day comes when You choose to show me Your purposes. Until then, give me grace to trust You completely. Amen."*

The Problem With Pain
DAY 5: HOW AM I GOING TO RESPOND?

Briefly describe a challenge or trial that you are currently facing.

Are you able to discern whether the origin of that adversity is the result of personal sin; is an attack by Satan, or whether it originated with God?

Does knowing the source of the adversity affect the way in which you are responding to this trial?

Week 1: The Problem with Pain

How will you respond differently to adversity from each of the following?

- sin:

- Satan

- God

Do you believe that God is in control and has allowed this trial to enter into your life for a purpose?

When Something Painful Happens....

"Something painful happened to me. This is how I met it:
I was quiet for a while with the Lord, and then
I wrote these words for myself:

'First, He brought me here. It is by His will I am in this strait place:
in that fact I will rest.
Next, He will keep me here in His love,
and give me grace as His child.

Then, He will make the trial a blessing, teaching me the lessons
He intends me to learn, and working in me
the grace He needs to bestow.

Last, in His good time He can bring me out again –
how and when only He knows. Let me say I am here,
first, by God's appointment;
Second, in His keeping;
Third, under His training;
Fourth, for His time."

(From Dr. V. Raymond Edman; "In Quiet and Confidence")

Facing Adversity

Have you thanked the Lord for accomplishing His will in your life, even if it involves allowing pain? Take a moment now and write out a prayer of thanksgiving to Him.

WEEK 2

Putting Adversity into Perspective
DAY 1: WHY IS GOD ALLOWING THIS?

Have you ever thought, *If God knows about my troubles, why has He allowed them to come into my life? Doesn't He love me?*

While human reasoning says that all suffering is to be avoided, God's Word reveals that He has a purpose in allowing our pain. We need to see the *big picture*, God's perspective on the events and circumstances of our lives.

Adversity can be one of God's greatest tools in building our lives. The trials that He allows to enter our lives are designed not to destroy us, but to build us; they are not to be seen as a blight, but viewed as an opportunity for tremendous blessing.

What does Scripture say about adversity's "positive side?"

1.   II Corinthians 4:17, 18

Facing Adversity

2. James 1:2-4

3. James 1:12

4. Romans 5:3-5

5. I Peter 4:13, 14

The real question in dealing victoriously with adversity is "How should I respond to this?" As in all of life, we are to "have this attitude yourselves which was also in Christ Jesus" (Philippians 2:5). Having the Scriptural perspective on life's troubles is possible since we know that "we have the mind of Christ" (I Corinthians 2:16).

The foundational building block in our perspective on adversity is having an accurate understanding of who God is. We may ask, "Why doesn't God change this situation? Isn't He powerful enough to stop the pain?"

Look up the following references and record your insights regarding God's character.

A. GOD IS SOVEREIGN

6. Isaiah 14:24, 27

7. Psalm 31:15

Week 2: Putting Adversity into Perspective

8. Psalm 139:16

How does knowing that God is in control of your life affect your perspective on life?

God has complete power over everything. He is the absolute Ruler of all, including every detail of our lives. But that would not be good news if we worshipped a god who was cruel or mean-spirited. What does Scripture reveal about the heart of God?

B. GOD IS GOOD AND CARES ABOUT US

9. Psalm 56:8-13

10. Isaiah 49:14-16

11. Lamentations 3:31-33

Have you ever felt that God has forgotten you? Based on Isaiah 49:14-16, why would God remember you and what you are going through?

God is not like one who says, "Don't worry, you'll get over it." He is personally involved and deeply cares about each one of us. But what if we worshipped a god who was in control and well-intentioned, yet failed to take action on our behalf? What does Scripture reveal about the actions of God?

Facing Adversity

C.   GOD IS POWERFUL

12.   Psalm 57:2

13.   Jeremiah 29:11

14.   Romans 8:28

15.   Ephesians 3:20   How much is God able to do for us?

Praise the Lord, our wonderful God is not only sovereign and caring; He always works mightily on our behalf to accomplish His best!

> *"Thank You, Lord, for being in control of every detail of my life. I know that You love me and that great good is going to come out of this painful experience that I'm going through. Help me to keep my eyes on You during the coming days, because I trust You, Lord! Amen."*

Putting Adversity into Perspective
DAY 2: SEEING THE "BIG PICTURE"

Paul tells us that the Old Testament was written for our instruction to give us encouragement and hope (Romans 15:4). All Scripture trains us to be mature and equipped for life (II Timothy 3:16, 17). Throughout the Bible God has recorded stories of adversity and how various individuals have responded to trials.

Week 2: Putting Adversity into Perspective

Joseph was a man who endured a series of tremendous personal setbacks in life. In order to gain insight into the *big picture* (possibly God's perspective), let's look closely at his life.

1.   Genesis 37:1-36

Record your insights regarding the following areas of Joseph's family background and childhood:

      a.   Relationship with parents -

      b.   Birth order -

      c.   Relationship with siblings -

      d.   Basic home environment and attitudes -

      e.   Personal rights and freedom -

Did Joseph have cause to be bitter?

Under similar circumstances, how would you have reacted?

2.   Genesis 39:1-20

      a.   What evidence do you see of God blessing Joseph?

      b.   What happened in Potiphar's house?

Facing Adversity

    c.   Where did Joseph end up? (Also see Psalm 105:16-19)

Did Joseph have cause to be bitter?

Under similar circumstances, how would you have reacted?

3.   Genesis 39:21 - 40:23.

    a.   What evidence do you see of God blessing Joseph?

    b.   What happened to Joseph in jail?

    c.   Where did Joseph end up?

Did Joseph have cause to be bitter?

Under similar circumstances, how would you have reacted?

4.   Genesis 41:1-52.

    a.   What evidence do you see of God blessing Joseph?

    b.   Where did Joseph end up?

    After 13 years of misery what attitude did Joseph maintain?

Week 2: Putting Adversity into Perspective

5. Genesis 41:53-45:28

   a. Had Joseph's brothers changed in the preceding years? On what do you base your conclusion?

   b. Was Joseph bitter toward them?

   c. What did Joseph perceive to be the origin of his ample adversity? (Genesis 45:5-9; 50:20)

   d. What adjectives would you use to describe the events of Joseph's life if you had lived them?

   e. Can you locate any negative quotes or comments about Joseph in Scripture?

   f. What blessings were a result of Joseph's trials? Who was blessed?

Joseph was able to recognize God's hand working through the worst circumstances of life. Do you see the Lord's hand at work through the painful episodes of your life?

Have you ever seen from past experience that something which appeared to be "bad" actually turned out to be "good" for you? Describe that situation on another page or in the space below.

Facing Adversity

"THE WEAVER"

My life is but a weaving between my Lord and me,
I cannot choose the colors He worketh steadily.
Oftimes He weaveth sorrow, and I in foolish pride
Forget He sees the upper, and I, the underside.

Not 'til the loom is silent and the shuttles cease to fly
Shall God unroll the canvas and explain the reason why.
The dark threads are as needful in the Weaver's skillful hand
As the threads of gold and silver in the pattern He has planned.
(author unknown)

"Father, it boggles my mind to see how You can use even the worst of circumstances to bring great good into our lives. You are an amazing God! You love me just like You loved Joseph, and I want to follow You every step of the way as You unfold the beautiful plan that You have for my life. Thank You, Jesus. Amen."

Putting Adversity into Perspective
DAY 3: WHY DOESN'T GOD FIX THIS?

Yesterday we saw how God used one man's lifetime of trials to ultimately accomplish something wonderful for many people. The *big picture* of Joseph's life revealed a beautiful plan of God's love and provision.

Today we will look at another biblical account in which several individuals experienced a time of great personal pain.

1.   John 11:1-45.

      a.   What was Jesus' relationship to Mary, Martha, and Lazarus?

Week 2: Putting Adversity into Perspective

b. Describe the problem/trouble.

c. Why do you think that Jesus delayed responding to the call for help?

d. How do you think that the disciples felt when Jesus said that His dear friend was dead and that He was glad that He wasn't there in time to save him?

e. Why did Jesus weep? (Also see Hebrews 4:15)

f. Which characters in this story were undergoing adversity?

g. Was there a purpose to this adversity? If so, what was that purpose?

h. Do we have any evidence that the purpose for this adversity was accomplished or fulfilled?

God's purpose was not to cause pain for Joseph, Mary, or Martha. His purpose was not to cause death for Lazarus. God hurts when we hurt, but some things are so important to Him that He will interrupt our comfort in order to accomplish them.

Joseph patiently endured his trials and had God's perspective on his pain. Mary and Martha were unable to see the *big picture* until Jesus revealed it to them. Being able to see beyond our immediate pain is a key to persevering with victory.

Facing Adversity

"Wisdom" has been defined as "the ability to see life from God's point of view." During times of duress, we need to ask the Lord to reveal to us, through the Holy Spirit, God's perspective on what is happening.

Have you ever felt that God was *silent* or *slow to answer* when you cried to Him for help? How did you respond?

How do you think that you should respond when there are periods of silence, or when it appears that God has forgotten you?

Consider a trial or difficulty that you are currently facing. Can you discern what God's perspective might be on this situation? How might the Lord use this "negative" experience to accomplish His "positive" purposes?

> *"Oh Father, Your plans are so intricately glorious! Thank You for having such a perfect design for my life. You are my Good Shepherd and You have led me to the place where I am today. Even though I can't see everything that You're doing right now, I believe that You're doing something wonderful through this trial that I'm facing. Be glorified in my life, Lord. I love You! Amen."*

Putting Adversity into Perspective
DAY 4: GETTING OUR ATTENTION

The Lord longs to have an intimate relationship with us. He "opens His hand, and satisfies the desire of every living thing" and our Lord is "kind in all His deeds" (Psalm 145:16, 17). His desire is always for our good; yet, often we do not cooperate with Him.

God may allow adversity to enter into our lives in order to get our attention. We tend to more readily call upon Him and listen for His voice when we are in need. The Lord will

Week 2: Putting Adversity into Perspective

turn the heat up in our lives in order to cause us to focus on Him. Because He loves us, God will custom-design our adversity to be as intense as necessary.

1. Acts 9:1-8.

    a. How did God get Saul's (Paul's) attention?

    b. Would you consider this as being an extreme step to take to get his attention?

    c. Why do you think that God took such a dramatic steps with Saul? (Also read Acts 9:15, 16)

    d. How did Saul respond to this adversity?

    e. When Saul listened, what did he hear?

Remember, our personal trials are uniquely designed by God to communicate individually with us. Even though Saul's encounter was witnessed by others on the Damascus Road, only Saul understood Jesus' voice speaking (Acts 22:9). Likewise, there may be times when we experience painful circumstances, while those around us do not fully appreciate the depth or gravity of what the Lord is doing in our lives.

    f. Did Saul act upon what he heard?

The Lord will allow our trials to be as intense as necessary in order to get our attention. He will also allow those trials be painful enough to shift our focus onto God Himself. Adversity hurts.

Facing Adversity

2. Job 3:11, 12, 20, 23

   Describe the feelings that Job had during his painful hours.

3. Job 6:8, 9

   Have you ever experienced the type of response that Job had in these verses?

When the pain that we experience is beyond our ability to control, we are prompted to cry out to the Lord in the right ways. David cried out to God "all day long" (Psalm 86:3.) During the throes of pain we cry out to the Lord with our voice (Psalm 3:4), and He hears us if we cry with a pure heart (Psalm 66:18).

Much as the intensity of the cry of a child will determine how quickly the parent will respond, our Lord hears us and "He does not forget the cry of the afflicted" (Psalm 9:12).

During the turbulent storms of life we are tempted to think that God does not hear us. Yet, it is very possible that during our times of thunder (described in Psalm 81:7) that God is most easily found (Psalm 81:7). We cry out to Him, though He is not clearly visible. He is there waiting for us. He is trying to get our attention. He is listening for us to call His name.

Saul (Paul) was an unbeliever who met God through adversity. Job was a righteous man who grew closer to God through adversity. Tomorrow we will meet others who were impacted by the trials that God allowed into their lives.

> *"God whispers to us in our pleasures, speaks in our conscience*
> *but shouts in our pains: it is His megaphone to rouse*
> *a deaf world."   (C.S. Lewis)*

Week 2: Putting Adversity into Perspective

Lord, You alone are the Almighty God. I'm so privileged to be Your child! Father, the deep desire of my heart is to have a consistent and close relationship with You. But, I have to confess that I am prone to wander away from Your side. I'm so easily distracted by the cares and demands of my daily life. Forgive me, Lord. Thank You for never giving up on me, and for using this adversity that I'm facing to get my attention. Amen."

Putting Adversity into Perspective
DAY 5: REFOCUSING

Yesterday we saw how God uses adversity to get the attention of people from diverse spiritual backgrounds. He used adversity to get Paul's attention even though he was a violent persecutor of God's people, and He used affliction to get Job's attention even though he was a righteous and godly man. The Lord drew each of these men closer to Himself through their unique trials.

The presence, or absence, of adversity in a person's life does not indicate the condition of one's spiritual health. However, today we will see how the speed with which we respond to the Lord by giving Him our complete attention does indicate our spiritual health.

We have seen that adversity stops us and causes us to refocus our attention. The question is; on what do we refocus? Do we scurry about looking for our own solutions to ease our pain, or do we run to the Lord and look into His face?

Jonah was a man who was running away from God. The Lord instructed him to "go to Ninevah" and tell the inhabitants of God's impending judgment (Jonah 1:2). Jonah's immediate response was to set his eyes toward Tarshish, the opposite direction (1:3).

1. Jonah 2:1-9

    a. To where did Jonah refocus his attention during his pain?

Facing Adversity

      b.   What evidence do you see that through this adversity Jonah rededicated his life to God?

We read in Scripture that the Lord appointed a "whale" of an adversity to stop him (Jonah 1:17). While Jonah was inside of the fish his attention was refocused upon God.

2.   II Chronicles 20:1-13

In this passage Israel is crying out to God for deliverance from her enemies.

      a.   According to verse three what motivated Jehoshaphat to focus his attention on seeking the Lord?

      b.   In verse twelve the nation turns their eyes to the Lord. What drove Israel to finally focus on God?

We all need to keep our focus sharpened on the Lord so that we can accurately see Jesus and see the truth about ourselves from His perspective. Sadly, without realizing it, well-meaning believers can easily become distracted and lose their focus on the Lord.

3.   Deuteronomy 8:7-14

      a.   What types of things can cause us to forget the Lord?

      b.   Have you ever seen this to be true in your own life?

The Lord uses all kinds of adversity, challenges and difficulties to get our attention; to cause us to refocus on Himself. When we come to the end of our own power and ideas; when we finally reach the bottom, the end of our rope, that is the time that we tend to reach out to Jesus.

Week 2: Putting Adversity into Perspective

How merciful and loving of Him to go to all of that work in order to hold our hand. It has been said that if the breeze of adversity doesn't get our attention, then God sends wind. If the wind is ignored, God sends a storm. Finally, He will get our attention with a whirlwind if necessary. Do you tend to respond quickly to the Lord when He wants your attention?

Can you recall a time of trial when you realize that the Lord was stopping you in your tracks to get your attention? Describe that event and your response to it.

"God's stiffest competition for our time, attention, and affections are the cares of this world. They choke out the Word of God and drown out the voice of God through His Holy Spirit (Matthew 13:18-23).

When adversity comes, we are suddenly faced with problems and pressures too big for us to resolve. That is when our inward response should be to call upon God. He has our attention!" (Bill Gothard)

"Heavenly Father, I'm beginning to see how You are using this pressure and difficulty in my life to nudge me back into Your arms. Oh, I love being near You, Father. Thank You for helping me to refocus on You. Nothing is sweeter than looking into Your face. Draw me close to You and never let me go! Amen."

Facing Adversity

WEEK 3

The Positive Side of Negative
DAY 1: GOD LOVES ME

The lives of people in the Bible demonstrate the fact that God uses adversity to accomplish His goals in people's lives, and that He "causes all things to work together for good" for those who love Him (Romans 8:28).

Initially, the Lord allows pain into our lives in order to sharpen our focus on Him. Once He has our attention, He can teach us and we can experience intimacy with Him. God, in His grace and mercy, allows Himself to be found by us when we seek Him diligently (Jeremiah 29:14). He promises to reveal Himself to us as we obediently walk with Him (John 14:21).

Though it is often difficult for us to discern His purposes while we are in the middle of a deep valley, the Lord encourages us to ponder pain's potential purposes. Our Creator wants us to cooperate with Him as the Holy Spirit works in our lives to conform us to the image of Christ (Romans 8:29).

Though God may not always let us see His purposes, He wants us to seek His heart.

God's Word sheds light upon various ways that the Lord uses trouble in our lives to glorify Himself through making us more like Christ. There is indeed a positive side of the

Facing Adversity

negative. God is accomplishing something through the trials that we endure. Our pain is not meaningless or wasted.

Throughout this study we will discover that there are five basic principles at work through our suffering:

I. Adversity enables us to see God. Last week we saw how the Lord uses adversity to get our attention so that He can remind us of His great love and faithfulness in our lives.

II. Adversity enables us to see ourselves. This week we will see how trials enable us to examine our lives so that we can see ourselves more accurately.

III. Adversity provides a platform for spiritual growth. In Week 5 we will discover how adversity exposes our personal weaknesses so that our faith can grow and become purified as we learn to depend upon God.

IV. Adversity clarifies our purpose in life. During Week 6 we will see how the Lord uses times of trial to clear the clutter from our lives in order to define, and refine, our true priorities.

V. Adversity prepares us for blessing. In Week 7 we will learn how God equips us for a ministry of comforting others, and see the role that adversity plays as God prepares us for an eternity of future reward.

Today we will focus on the great truth that adversity enables us to see God by reminding us of His love for us. As believers, we know that God is good and He loves us. He does not afflict or grieve men willingly (Lamentations 3:31-33). He has a plan for our lives springing from His great love for us (Jeremiah 29:11). Yet, during times of pain, Satan tries to convince us that God has forsaken us.

1. Hebrews 12:5-11.

    a. When we are being reproved or disciplined by the Lord, what does it prove?

    b. How does God show His legal (not illigitimate) ownership of us?

Week 3: The Positive Side of Negative

c. How does God's discipline in our lives affect our relationship with Him in verses 9 - 10?

d. Does God intend for discipline to hurt? Why?

e. What is the ultimate purpose of God's discipline?

f. Can you recall a time in your life when you were going through difficulty that you now realize was God's discipline or correction in your life?

If so, describe the events of that "training session."

Did you sense God's love when you were being chastened?

Afterwards, did you see that the Lord gave you a greater respect for Himself, and enabled you to live more righteously?

Do you perceive God's love now as you view His chastening in retrospect?

J. Vernon McGee told the story of his being "switched" by his school principal when he was a youngster. Just before he was to receive his discipline he was advised by one of the older children, "As you're being whipped, take a step toward him; because the closer you get, the less it will hurt."

Facing Adversity

When you're experiencing the Lord's discipline, do you tend to step closer to God or move farther away? It will always hurt less if we will move closer to Jesus.

"Adversity can be our greatest motivation for spiritual growth or our deadliest means of discouragement. The difference depends on our understanding of God's purposes through adversity." (Bill Gothard)

Take a moment and thank the Lord right now for the love He has demonstrated in your life through disciplining you as His child. Confess to Him any areas in which you have failed to cooperate with Him during times of chastening, and commit to Him that it is your heart's desire to step closer to Him as He trains you in the future. Write your prayer in the space below.

The Positive Side of Negative
DAY 2: GOD IS GENTLE WITH ME

When God allows any type of adversity into our lives, it is not only purposeful, it is also custom-designed by our loving Father. We are individually unique and God tailors the way He trains and teaches us. He specifically and gently accomplishes what is best for us without destroying or harming us.

Week 3: The Positive Side of Negative

1. Isaiah 28:23-29.

    a. Are all crops planted identically? (verse 25)

    b. How are these crops harvested? (verses 27, 28)

    c. If you were "dill, cumin, or grain" would you consider harvest time to be painful?

    d. Why does the farmer limit the length of time that He threshes? (verse 28)

God does not want to damage us. He loves us. Yet, in order to harvest the "fruit of the Spirit" in our lives (Galatians 5:22, 23), He lovingly may apply pain. The results bring glory to the Lord and make us useful to God.

2. Romans 8:28, 29

    What God has predestined us to become?

The great artist Michelangelo was a master-sculptor. Tradition states that when asked how he went about creating his marble statue of David, he replied that he simply took a huge chunk of marble and chiseled off everything that didn't look like David.

In a similar way, God uses His discipline to cut everything off of our lives that doesn't look like Christ. There may be pain in the cutting, but the results are glorious.

Facing Adversity

3. Psalm 46:1

   During trouble, what does God Himself do for us?

"My Own"
(Judy Gerry)

I know every bird of the mountains.	*(Psalm 50:11)*
All that moves in the meadow is Mine;	*(Deuteronomy 22:6, 7)*
Involved in each life I am counting -	*(Matthew 10:30)*
Compassionate, loving and kind.	*(Psalm 145:16, 17)*
I placed all the stars in the heavens,	*(Psalm 147:4)*
I numbered and measured each light.	*(Jeremiah 31:37)*
With care each a name has been given.	*(Psalm 147:4)*
In love they illumine the night.	*(Psalm 136:9)*
So why cry this strange accusation	
That you are abandoned, alone?	*(Matthew 28:20)*
Concerned for each bit of Creation,	*(Matthew 10:29-31)*
I tenderly nurture My own.	*(Isaiah 49:14-16)*
Just watch the birds fly in the morning	*(Psalm 50:11)*
And see the stars wink in the night.	*(Jeremiah 31:35)*
View nature as objects for learning	*(Matthew 6:26-33)*
You can trust Me with all of your life.	*(Psalm 71:5, 6)*

"Thank You my Father, for being my strong refuge. I know that I can run to You when life seems overwhelming and that You will protect me from anything that will destroy me. Thank you for tenderly dealing with me when I am hurting and fearful; for gently caring about every detail of my life. I know that I can trust You with everything, and that You will always there to help me. Hallelujah! Amen."

Week 3: The Positive Side of Negative

The Positive Side of Negative
DAY 3: GOD NURTURES ME

1. John 15:1, 2

    a. Who is the vine?

    b. Who is the vinedresser?

    c. Who is the branch?

    d. What happens to the fruitful branch?

    e. Why does the vinedresser do this to the branch?

God has great plans for our lives! He wants the best for us. Because God loves us, He wants us to bear much fruit as His children (John 15:8, 9), and in order for us to bear fruit we must be occasionally "pruned."

While we theoretically understand that pruning is essential for the health and productivity of a vine, the process of being pruned may initially sound (and actually be) painful to us.

2. Ephesians 5:3-5, 11

    a. According to this passage, what types of "unfruitful" things need to be pruned from our lives?

Facing Adversity

Have you ever experienced pain as the Lord removed unfruitful things, unfruitful relationships, or fruitless activities from your life?

If so, describe one of those situations.

3. Matthew 13:22

   a. What types of things can choke out the "fruitfulness" of God's Word in a persons's life?

   Have you ever experienced pain as these things were taken away from you?

It is important to understand that pruning is an act of love on the part of the vinedresser. An old Scotch proverb states; "The Father is never so close to the branches as when he is trimming them." When our loving Lord prunes our lives it is always a gentle act of love.

The question that we must ask ourselves is "How will I respond to God's pruning process in my life?"

As you look at trials and adversity in your life, can you see where the Lord has used those seasons of pain to cut away those things that hindered your relationship with Jesus? If so, thank the Lord now for His loving care over you.

"Lord, I confess that I tend to get attached to all of the comfortable things in my life. I shouldn't, but I do. Forgive me, Father. I want my life to be fruitful and useful to You, so I'm asking You to give me a heart that doesn't resist You when You come to me with those pruning shears. Today, I lay myself open to You and ask that You will cut away anything from my life that will cause me to be less than what You want me to be. Thank You, Lord. Amen."

Week 3: The Positive Side of Negative

The Positive Side of Negative

DAY 4: GOD IS FATIHFUL TO ME

We can count on God's love and presence in our lives continually. A true friend stands by you when life gets difficult, and Jesus calls us His friends (John 15:15, 16).

When life is going smoothly we can reason intellectually that God is faithful. Our theology can be perfect. We may theoretically understand that God is Who He says He is.

But when adversity strikes we are able to experience first hand God's faithfulness in our lives. Our theories become tangible as the Lord personally carries us through the storm. As a result of walking through the storm with the Lord, we not only mentally know that God is faithful, we also "know it by heart."

When we are in the middle of a painful episode in life, we need to be continually reminded of three principles regarding God's faithfulness.

A.   GOD IS ALWAYS FAITHFUL.

In the following verses note the conditions of God's faithfulness.

1.   II Timothy 2:13

2.   Psalm 119:75

Our wonderful Lord is always faithful to us through the trials of life. He is faithful in His attitude toward us, His actions toward us, and He faithfully works on our behalf during times of duress.

B.   GOD'S FAITHFULNESS OFTEN DELIVERS US **FROM** ADVERSITY.

1.   Psalm 34:4, 6-7, 19

Facing Adversity

a. List all of the things from which God faithfully delivers us.

b. As you read the above passage, was the psalmist responsible to meet any conditions in order to experience the Lord's deliverance during his trials? If so, list those conditions in the space below.

Would you say that you are quick to respond to the Lord this way during your own personal times of adversity?

The Lord loves to carry us through adversity because He carries us close to Him. God tells us in Isaiah 46:3,4 that He has carried us from the womb and even through our old age. He says, "I will bear you! I have done it, and I will carry you; and I will bear you, and I will deliver you." He carries us through our trials, holding us close to His heart.

The Lord can quickly deliver us from our troubles, but He often allows our trials to endure for a long time. As we cling to Jesus, He continues to demonstrate His faithfulness to us during those seemingly endless days. Though the Lord has not promised to keep us from stormy seas, He has promised that He will always bring us to safe harbor.

C. GOD'S FAITHFULNESS ALWAYS SUSTAINS US **THROUGH** ADVERSITY.

2. Psalm 23:1-5

List all of the circumstances through which God sustains us.

Week 3: The Positive Side of Negative

3. Isaiah 43:2

   What will God do for us?

4. Hebrews 4:16

   What are we to do in times of need?

WHAT GOD SAYS TO US DURING OUR TRIALS   (Original source unknown)

You say:	"It's impossible."
God says:	All things are possible (Luke 18:27).
You say:	"I'm too tired."
God says:	I will give you rest (Matthew 11:28-30).
You say:	"Nobody really loves me."
God says:	I love you (John 3:16; 13:34).
You say:	"I can't go on."
God says:	My grace is sufficient (II Corinthians 12:9; Psalm 91:15).
You say:	"I can't figure things out."
God says:	I will direct your steps (Proverbs 3:5, 6).
You say:	"I can't do it."
God says:	You can do all things through Christ (Philippians 4:13).
You say:	"I'm not able."
God says:	I am able (II Corinthians 9:8).
You say:	"It's not worth it."
God says:	It will be worth it (Romans 8:28).

Facing Adversity

You say:	"I can't forgive myself."
God says:	I forgive you (I John 1:9; Romans 8:1).
You say:	"I can't manage."
God says:	I will supply all your needs (Philippians 4:19).
You say:	"I'm afraid."
God says:	I have not given you a spirit of fear (II Timothy 1:7).
You say:	"I'm always worried and frustrated."
God says:	Cast all your cares on ME (I Peter 5:7).
You say:	"I'm not smart enough."
God says:	I give you wisdom (I Corinthians 1:30).
You say:	"I feel all alone."
God says:	I will never leave you or forsake you (Hebrews 13:5).

("God says" are paraphrased)

"I'm clinging to You today, Jesus. There are days when life seems unbearable, and problems look unsolvable. But You are able to do exceedingly abundantly more that I can ask or think. You are more powerful than I can imagine. When I cry out to You, You are there. When I seek You, You show Yourself to me. How wonderful You are! You are so faithful and I know that You are able to handle every challenge of my life. Thank You, Jesus! Amen."

The Positive Side of Negative

DAY 5: REMEMBERING GOD'S PAST FAITHFULNESS

1. Lamentations 3:16-18

    Describe the emotional and spiritual state of this suffering prophet.

Week 3: The Positive Side of Negative

2. Lamentations 3:21-25

   What brought this prophet back into a state of hope in the Lord?

Every trial presents an opportunity for us to refocus our hearts and minds on the Lord. It brings God great glory and it brings us great peace when we remember how God has been faithful in the past. Recounting our previous experiences with Him will encourage our hearts.

Remembering God's past faithfulness in our lives not only builds us spiritually, it can also encourage others.

3. Psalm 71:17-20

   What does the psalmist declare to the future generations?

If we neglect to tell our children or others about the faithfulness that God has demonstrated in the past, then they may suffer. Read the verses below and record what happens if we are silent about the Lord.

4. Psalm 78:11

5. Psalm 78:22

6. Psalm 78:42

Facing Adversity

Each time that we experience God's faithfulness during adversity, we must scoop up that experience and put it on display for others to see. It will encourage us, our children, and others to "put their confidence in God" (Psalm 78:7).

As Jeremiah did in Lamentations, take time to recall to your mind the faithfulness of God. Make a detailed list of various episodes of adversity in your life and how God demonstrated His faithfulness to you during that time.

Date	Description of Adversity	God's Faithfulness

Week 3: The Positive Side of Negative

Date	Description of Adversity	God's Faithfulness

"Oh, You are such a Good Shepherd to me. As I look back over the path where You have led me in life, I can see how You have always taken such tender care of me. There are many days when I can't see the path in front of me, Lord, so thank You for the reassurance that You will lead me in the future as You have in the past. How faithful you are! As I face tomorrow, give me grace to follow You every step of the way. Amen."

Facing Adversity

WEEK 4

Adversity Enables Us to See Ourselves
DAY 1: AM I HARBORING UNCONFESSED SIN?

We have seen how the Lord can use the painful episodes of our lives to get our attention and cause us to focus on Him. As we look to God during times of trial we come face to face with our Lord who is sovereign, loving and faithful. Through the adversity we are able to see more clearly what is true about God Himself.

Adversity also helps us to discover what is true about ourselves. The Lord often uses adversity in our lives to reveal sins that we need to confess and forsake.

In the lives of all believers, the Holy Spirit points out ever deepening levels of disobedience so that we can repent of our sinful actions and attitudes. In addition to flagrant sin, the Lord wants to expose and deal with any wrong attitudes and ideas that may be nesting in our hearts (such as pride, prejudices, selfishness, materialism, anger, bitterness, jealously, grudges, etc.).

Often, we are unaware that these problems even exist. God uses adversity to force us to deal with things on a deeper level, and to honestly see ourselves as He sees us. It is at this point in our spiritual life that we really grow in our relationship with God and others.

Facing Adversity

When the winds of adversity pick up in our lives, we are to examine our hearts, not just our actions. We are to ask, "Am I in God's will? Is there any unconfessed sin in my life? What are You trying to tell me, God?"

"Examine me, O Lord, and try me; test my mind and my heart" (Psalm 26:2).

While not all suffering is the result of personal sin (I Peter 4:19), this should be the first area that we scrutinize when the flames of adversity ignite around us.

Difficult times that result from our sin are designed by God to lead us to repentance. It has been said that most people don't change because they see the light, but because they feel the heat.

During adversity God turns up the heat to induce us to change. The first step in changing is to recognize the existence of our sin.

Look up the following verses and note any relationship between an individual's suffering and their personal sin.

1. Luke 1:20

2. Acts 12:21-23

3. Psalm 107:17

4. II Chronicles 7:22

5. I Corinthians 11:19-30

Week 4: Adversity Enables Us to See Ourselves

    a.   What wrong attitudes and actions were evident in the Corinthian church?

    b.   What adversity was the church experiencing because of "sin in the ranks (verses 19, 30)?"

    c.   In order to avoid condemnation along with the world, what were the believers exhorted to do?

Adversity should stimulate us to examine ourselves.

6.   II Corinthians 13:5

    In what area are we to test ourselves?

Since we are not always able to see our own sin, adversity should prompt us to lay ourselves open to the scrutiny of God Himself. We need the Holy Spirit's help in order to truly discern any sin in our lives. Only God knows our heart (Jeremiah 17:9,10). We may justify our actions, but it is the Lord who examines the hidden places of our soul (I Thessalonians 2:4).

In the following verses, what does Job examine in his life?

7.   Job 7:17-20

8.   Job 13:23

Facing Adversity

Do you discern that some of the adversity that you have endured in the past, or that you may be experiencing right now, may be the result of sin in your life?

It is important for us to remember that God is abundant in His love. He is so merciful that even when we experience pain as a result of our sin, that pain is always less than we deserve (Psalm 103:10).

Since our hearts are deceitful and desperately sick, and only the Lord can reveal the truth about us, have you asked Christ to show you any hidden sin in your life? Take some time right now and talk to the Lord about your desire to see what He sees when He looks into your heart.

"Lord, Your Word says that people sometimes experience adversity as a direct result of their personal sin. I want to be sure that I haven't sinned against You, Father. Please show me any area of my life where I might have allowed some bad attitude, thought, or action to nest in my heart. I don't want to harbor anything that will separate me from You, so examine me, Lord. Show me the truth about me. Amen."

Adversity Enables Us to See Ourselves
DAY 2: AM I WILLING TO REPENT?

When the Lord shows us any area of sin in our lives, it is God's invitation for us to draw near and be taught by His Holy Spirit. It is during those storms of adversity that the Lord wants us to cultivate teachable hearts. From the following passages, how do we display a responsiveness to God?

Week 4: Adversity Enables Us to See Ourselves

Verses	What are we warned against?	How do we demonstrate a teachable heart?
Psalm 139:23, 24		
Job 6:24		
Lamentations 3:39-42		

4. Read Hebrews 12:15

   a. What warning is given in this passage?

   b. Verse 15 immediately follows a discussion of God's discipline of His children. Do you think there might be any correlation between discipline and the warning given in verse 15? Explain.

   c. Have you ever been ensnared by a bitter heart while undergoing the discipline of the Lord? If so, stop now and examine yourself, asking the Lord for forgiveness.

Facing Adversity

Remember, Godly self-examination during our trials yields great benefit.

5.   Psalm 119:67, 71

   How can affliction benefit your life?

6.   James 1:14, 15

   What is the result of unchecked sin?

When our sin is revealed to us, we can become paralyzed with shock and discouragement. We may tempted to grieve that sin with a defeated spirit. We may weep and wail over our sin. Yet, how does the Lord want us to respond when He reveals sin in our lives?

7.   II Corinthians 7:9, 10

   Just "feeling sorry" about our sin is not enough. What does "godly sorrow" produce?

Are you willing to repent of any sin that the Lord may reveal to you?

Pain is a great protector in life. Without the sharp, persistent warning of danger, we might continue to do the same harmful thing, resulting in severe damage to ourselves. The pain of adversity is designed to bring us to repentance. God promises to forgive us when we repent (I John 1:9).

8.   II Kings 22:19, 20

   What resulted from Josiah's repentance for the nation?

Week 4: Adversity Enables Us to See Ourselves

9.   Proverbs 28:13

What does the Lord promise to those who repent?

Are you willing to forsake your hidden sin if the Lord shows it to you? (Consider areas such as grudges, bitterness, anger, jealousy, greed, etc.)

    If no, why not?

Are you willing to invest time and energy searching the Scriptures so that the Holy Spirit can correct and teach you?

    If no, why not?

> *"I have set before you life and death, the blessing and the curse.*
> *So choose life in order that you may live, you and your descendants;*
> *by loving the Lord your God, by obeying His voice, and by holding fast to Him."*
> *(Deuteronomy 30:19, 20)*

Is any sin in your life worth holding onto in light of the curse or the blessing that God has promised? Examine yourself.

"Father, forgive me for taking my sin so lightly. I'm guilty of comparing myself with others and thinking that I'm 'not so bad.' But, You are holy, Lord. You love me too much to leave me to rot away in my subtle secret sins. Your love is too deep to leave me to drown in my overt wickedness. Show my sin to me, Lord, and I will repent. I want Your blessing. I want You! Amen."

Facing Adversity

Adversity Enables Us to See Ourselves

DAY 3: PRIDE—AN EVER-PRESENT DANGER

We know that through Jesus Christ God has a plan for those whom He loves that is for our good (Jeremiah 29:11). He wants us to be conformed to Christ's image (Romans 8:29) and to be "useful to the Master, prepared for every good work" (II Timothy 2:21). After all, "we are His workmanship, created in Christ Jesus for good works, which God prepared beforehand, that we should walk in them" (Ephesians 2:10).

Yet as we walk with the Lord, we face an enemy from within: our pride. Pride is an ever-present adversary of the believer. Satan was the originator of pride, as he said in his heart, "I will ascend to heaven, I will raise my throne above the stars of God, I will sit on the mount of the assembly ... I will ascend above the heights of the clouds; I will make myself like the Most High" (Isaiah 14:13, 14).

Pride is tantamount to seeing ourselves as God. Pride is idolatry. Pride is sin. And at the center of both "pride" and "sin" is the *almighty* "I." It is most readily detected when we find ourselves protecting "I." Whenever we begin to defend ourselves, we can be fairly certain that pride has reared its ugly head.

Pride describes the evil heart of Satan and it also describes the world. "The boastful pride of life is not from the Father, but is from the world" (I John 2:16).

God hates pride. Not only does the Lord call pride *sin*, He assures us that it will lead us to disaster. What do the following verses say about pride?

1. Proverbs 8:13

2. Proverbs 11:2

3. Proverbs 16:18

Week 4: Adversity Enables Us to See Ourselves

4.   Proverbs 21:4

As we yield to the Lord and He uses us, there is often a tendency to give the credit for the work to the individual rather than to God Himself. Note what the following verses say.

5.   Isaiah 48:11

6.   Isaiah 42:8

The Father desires for us to be like His Son and He lovingly works in us to eradicate pride. Very often He uses adversity to accomplish that goal. King Nebuchadnezzar of Babylon gives us a clear biblical example of man's pride.

7.   Daniel 4:30-37

   a.   What evidence of pride do you see?

   b.   What was the result of that pride?

   c.   What was the origin of Nebuchadnezzar's adversity?

   d.   What happened when Nebuchadnezzar raised his "eyes toward heaven?"

   e.   Would you say that God used adversity to conquer Nebuchadnezzar's pride?

Facing Adversity

Have you ever experienced a situation where you took credit for something God had done in your life? Describe that time. (Consider the areas of your family, wealth, economic status, spiritual maturity, educational opportunity, physical appearance, etc.)

How do you think that God felt about your taking the credit for what He has done?

Did the Lord send any adversity along to humble you? If so, describe that situation and record how you responded to that season of testing.

8. Read Psalm 115:1

   Is this the sincere prayer of your heart? How is it your prayer?

Week 4: Adversity Enables Us to See Ourselves

"Fingerprints"
(Judy Gerry)

Oh Lord, touch me.
As You protect me in Your palm - cover me.
As You direct my steps - nudge me with Your hand.
As You cradle me in Your arms - stroke my cheek.
As you take me through the valleys of my life - lead me by the hand.

Put Your fingerprints all over me, Father.
Put Your fingerprints all over the circumstances
and appointed times of my life.

Let me know the distinct power and gentleness of Your touch.
Let me recognize that it is Your hand
in my life guiding and directing;

So that I can be confident in those hours of confusion
when I need to know Who has led me.

So that I can take comfort in the fact that You are
the One meeting my needs.

So that others will know that You have been here
and look for Your hand.

So that You, alone, will get the glory due You.

Touch me, Abba.
Cover my life with Your fingerprints so that I can know,
and others can see, that You are here. [Selah]

"Lord Jesus, I realize that anything good in my life has come straight from You. Forgive me for those times when I have embezzled Your glory and hoarded it for myself. I joyfully give it all back to you, Lord. I fall on my face and join that heavenly choir singing, 'Worthy is the Lamb that was slain to receive power and riches and wisdom and might and honor and glory and blessing.' Hallelujah! Amen."

Facing Adversity

Adversity Enables Us to See Ourselves

DAY 4: ME? PROUD?

When we think of godly people in the Bible the apostle Paul comes to mind. Yet, Paul struggled greatly with his proud nature.

1. Philippians 3:4-6

    By the world's standards, did Paul have reason to be a proud person? Why, or why not?

2. II Corinthians 12:7

    a. Why could personal pride have been a stumbling block in Paul's life?

    b. What did God do to protect Paul from his pride?

3. II Corinthians 11:23-28

    What adversity did Paul suffer?

4. II Corinthians 1:8 and II Corinthians 4:8

    Was Paul ever overwhelmed by the intensity of the adversity "assigned" to him?

Week 4: Adversity Enables Us to See Ourselves

5.   II Corinthians 10:17, 18

   What is Paul's conclusion regarding personal pride?

As with all sin, we need the Holy Spirit to reveal to us what is true about our hearts (John 16:8). Pride is a slippery rascal; hiding where we cannot readily detect it and nestling into the hidden nooks and crannies of our hearts. It is a deceiver that justifies itself and even camouflages itself in the appearance of "pseudo-righteousness."

What does pride look like in our hearts? The opposite of pride is humility.

In her book, *Seeking Him* (co-authored with Tim Grissom), Nancy Leigh DeMoss contrasts the heart of proud people with the heart of humble people. Read the following pages and ask the Lord to reveal to you which characteristics of a proud heart are true of your own life. Put a checkmark beside any that you sense particularly relate to your own life.

- ❏   Proud people focus on the failures of others;
  Humble people are overwhelmed with a sense of their own spiritual need.

- ❏   Proud people have an independent self-sufficient spirit;
  Humble people have a dependent spirit, and recognize their need for others.

- ❏   Proud people have to prove they are right.;
  Humble people are willing to yield the right to be right.

- ❏   Proud people are self-righteous and critical;
  Humble people are compassionate; they can forgive much because they know how much they have been forgiven.

- ❏   Proud people are quick to blame others;
  Humble people accept personal responsibility and can see where they are wrong in a situation.

- ❏   Proud people are defensive when criticized;
  Humble people receive criticism with an open spirit.

- ❏   Proud people are self-conscious;
  Humble people are not concerned with self at all.

Facing Adversity

- [ ] Proud people want to be recognized and appreciated;
  Humble people have a sense of their own unworthiness, and are thrilled that God would use them at all in any ministry.

- [ ] Proud people compare themselves with others and feel worthy of honor;
  Humble people compare themselves to the holiness of God and feel a desperate need for His mercy.

- [ ] Proud people claim rights, and have a demanding spirit;
  Humble people are willing to yield their rights, and have a meek spirit.

- [ ] Proud people are self-protective of their time, their rights, and their reputation;
  Humble people are self-denying.

- [ ] Proud people tend to deal in generalities when confessing sin;
  Humble people, under the conviction of God's Spirit, are able to acknowledge specifics when confessing their sin.

- [ ] Proud people desire to be served;
  Humble people are motivated to serve others.

- [ ] Proud people desire to make a name for themselves;
  Humble people are motivated to be faithful and to make others a success.

- [ ] Proud people feel confident in how much they know;
  Humble people are humbled by how very much they have to learn.

- [ ] Proud people don't think they need revival, but are sure that everyone else does;
  Humble people continually sense their need for a fresh encounter with God and for a fresh filling of His Holy Spirit.

- [ ] Proud people keep others at arm's length;
  Humble people are willing to risk getting close to others and to take risks of loving intimately.

- [ ] Proud people are unapproachable;
  Humble people are easy to be entreated.

- [ ] Proud people find it difficult to share their spiritual needs with others;
  Humble people are willing to be open and transparent with others as God directs.

Week 4: Adversity Enables Us to See Ourselves

- ❏ Proud people have a hard time saying, "I was wrong; will you please forgive me?"
  Humble people are quick to admit failure and to seek forgiveness when necessary.

- ❏ Proud people are remorseful over their sin, sorry that they got found out or caught;
  Humble people are truly repentant over their sin; forsake their sin.

- ❏ Proud people wait for others to come and ask forgiveness when there is a misunderstanding or conflict in a relationship;
  Humble people take the initiative to be reconciled when there is a misunderstanding or a conflict in relationships; no matter how wrong the other may have been.

- ❏ Proud people are blind to their true heart condition;
  Humble people walk in the light.

- ❏ Proud people don't think they have anything to repent of;
  Humble people realize they have need of continual heart attitude of repentance.

- ❏ Proud people want to be sure that no one finds out when they have sinned; instinct is to cover up;
  Humble people are broken and don't care who knows or who finds out; are willing to be exposed because they have nothing to lose.

As you considered these descriptions of pride, in which specific areas did you most readily identify?

Paul had to deal with the pride in his life. Do you?

> ***"Oh my Savior, it's difficult for me to recognize my pride. I'm so used to listening to it, feeling it, and breathing it, that I can't even see it without your Holy Spirit revealing it to me. I want to repent, Father. Show me where my pride is ruling and give me the grace to quickly humble myself in that area. Begin Your work in me and do whatever is necessary to rid me of this monster who robs me of Your joy and blessing in life. Amen."***

Facing Adversity

Adversity Enables Us to See Ourselves

DAY 5: DEALING WITH MY PRIDE

Yesterday we learned that humility is the opposite of pride. What does the Lord give to the humble?

1.   James 4:6

2.   I Peter 5:5

   How does God relate to the proud person?

God promises to give grace to the humble. Not only are we saved by grace (Ephesians 2:8, 9), we also live by grace. Grace is, "the dynamic quality of God in me that gives me the desire and power to live in harmony with God and His word" (I Corinthians 15:10).

If we desire more of God's grace to be manifested in our lives, we know that we need more humility. But how do we become more humble? By nature we are unaware that we are proud people. We cannot discern our own pride without the Holy Spirit revealing it to us.

God may use adversity to humble the proud person. It has been said that, "we will either become humble people, or God will humble us." God faithfully works in our lives, but much is on the line based on how we respond to His promptings.

In the following verses, note the benefit that the Lord bestows on those who humble themselves:

3.   James 4:10

4.   I Peter 5:6, 7

Week 4: Adversity Enables Us to See Ourselves

Why do you think that the encouragement of verse 7 immediately follows the exhortation in verse 6?

Philippians 2:3, 4 tells us that the mind of humility is seen when we "regard one another as more important than (ourselves); not looking out for our own personal interests, but also for the interests of others." We are humble when we're cheering for the other person and wanting to put them in the best possible light.

An attitude of humility is evidenced when we genuinely desire and delight in the success of others; when we want the best for them without considering how we stack up; when we're willing to sacrifice ourselves for their good.

Christ is the ultimate example of humility.

5. Philippians 2:5-11

   a. What reason did Christ have to be boastful or proud?

   b. What did He do to "humble Himself?"

   c. Was adversity involved in His "humbling Himself?"

   d. Who gets the glory from Christ's self-humbling?

Very often adversity is the means by which the Holy Spirit points out areas of our pride. We must humble ourselves and confess our sin. When we renounce our pride we are then able to recognize our need and how much God has done in our lives.

Facing Adversity

"Jesus, You are the King of Kings, and yet You humbled Yourself by setting aside the honor and rights that were rightfully Yours. Oh Lord, I want to be like You. I want to humble myself, too. Thank you for the way that You are using the adversity and trials in my life to show me where I am jealously guarding my own self-proclaimed 'honor and rights.' Thank You for giving me this opportunity to identify my pride and to humble myself. Oh Lord, be glorified in my life and pour Your grace all over me! Amen."

WEEK 5

Adversity Teaches Us to Depend on God
DAY 1: THE SECRET OF BEING STRONG

Last week we saw the Lord deal with Paul's tendency toward pride through the application of adversity. Paul was humbled, though he had reason in the flesh to boast about himself. After his conversion, Paul boasted about two things. What were those two things?

1.   II Corinthians 11:30

2.   I Corinthians 1:31

Paul discovered the spiritual secret that *the area of our greatest weakness is where God can shine the brightest.* We tend to think that the Lord is most glorified in our lives through our areas of strength. Yet, just the opposite is true.

Our natural abilities are not necessarily what God will use, and our innate talents are not the measure of our spiritual giftedness or ability to serve the Lord.

Facing Adversity

In contemporary culture, strength and savvy are considered to be invaluable assets, but this is contrary to Scripture.

3. I Corinthians 1:26-29

    a. What does the Lord use?

    b. Why do you think that God has chosen to use these things?

In God's economy, weakness is a valuable commodity!

4. I Samuel 17:1-51

    a. Describe the strength of the Philistine.

    b. What status did David have in Israel?

    c. What status did David have in his family?

    d. How did King Saul try to "strengthen" David for the battle?

    e. What physical weapons did David take into battle?

Week 5: Adversity Teaches Us to Depend on God

    f.   Using human reasoning, how did the Philistine respond to the sight of "weak" David?

    g.   On what basis did David proclaim victory prior to the battle?

    h.   How did God use David's apparent weakness?

Though it sounds like a contradiction, Paul says, "When I am weak, then I am strong." How would you describe this to another person?

> *"When God works in power through our obvious weakness,
> both we and others are free to give Him all the praise."*
> (Bill Gothard)

"Lord, You are the powerful God who accomplishes anything good in my life. Father, You say that Your strength shines brightest in my life where I'm the weakest. But, I confess that I've tried to fluff up my own strengths and hide my weak areas. Forgive me Lord. I surrender to You, and am willing to look foolish to others and let them see my inadequacies so that You can shine through me. Let those around me see Your power and give You all the glory. This is my true heart's desire. Amen."

Facing Adversity

Adversity Teaches Us to Depend on God

DAY 2: RECOGNIZING MY OWN WEAKNESS

Our natural inclination is to hide or cover up areas of our weakness. Yet we see that God will often use adversity to specifically expose our weakest areas.

1. II Corinthians 12:1-10

    a. What evidence do you see here that Paul had received great spiritual knowledge and experience?

    b. Do you think that Paul purposed in his heart never to brag about any personal accomplishments?

    c. Did God see that Paul's pride was a continual obstacle in his life? On what basis do you conclude this?

    d. What did God allow in Paul's life to help him overcome his pride?

    (The word thorn = "skalops." It was a sharp, bungee stick, similar to a wooden stake.)

    Do you think that this was loving of God?

    e. How did Paul respond to this? Did he ask "why?" Did he ask that it be removed?

    Did God scold Paul for this response?

Week 5: Adversity Teaches Us to Depend on God

God does not design certain afflictions in our lives to weaken us, but His goal is to weaken our dependence on the flesh. He desires to weaken our hold onto our intellect, our personal strength, experience, education, eloquence, and natural abilities. When we let go of the world's ways we fall into the arms of Jesus.

When we begin to recognize our weakness we are forced to depend upon God.

Human reasoning says "when the going gets tough the tough get tougher." Yet in II Corinthians 12, Paul explains that when the going gets tough we need to acknowledge our weakness and affirm our absolute reliance on the Lord.

The Lord promises "abundant grace" (Romans 5:17) and He specifically promised Paul that He would be given enough grace to enable him to succeed (12:9).

2. II Corinthians 12:10

   a. What was Paul's final attitude toward weakness, insults, distress, persecutions and difficulties?

   b. According to this verse, whose reputation was on the line in Paul's weaknesses; for whose "sake" did Paul endure these adversities?

3. Philippians 4:11-13

   Was Paul born with a "Paul-lyanna" attitude regarding life, or was his contentment something that developed through experience?

   (The word for "learned" in 4:11 means "to learn by experience and practice; not innate.)

When the pressure of adversity is applied to our lives, our weakest points crack first. The ability to recognize and acknowledge our weaknesses is a blessing as we learn to lean on and draw our strength from the Lord Himself.

Facing Adversity

4. Has the Lord used adversity in your life to highlight your personal weaknesses? Explain the circumstances.

   Was your response one of "sweet resignation to the sovereignty and providence of God?"

   Have you "boasted" about your weakness so that He can get the glory from any success in your life?

   What "thorn" has the Lord placed in your life?

   Take time right now to stop, and thank God for your "thorn."

Your greatest weakness is God's greatest opportunity. When others see strength in the precise areas of your weakness and failure, Jesus gets all the glory. As we rely on Him for grace, the Lord does not merely give us the strength to "cope" with life's trials, He causes us to "overcome" victoriously.

> *"Does the circumstance press hard against you? Do not push it away. It is the Potter's hand. He is shaping you into a vessel of beauty and honor."* (author unknown)

Do you discern that some of the adversity in your life may be God working to conquer your pride? Describe the situation.

Week 5: Adversity Teaches Us to Depend on God

How have you responded to this adversity? Have you tried to run from it, push it away, force your way ahead or wriggle out of it? How does the Lord want you to respond?

"You are my Wonderful Counselor and I ask You to teach me today. I am feeling the sting of the 'thorn' that You have allowed into my life, but might You be using this 'thorn' as a tool to point out to me some area of weakness that I need to surrender to You? Lord, use this 'thorn' to penetrate my heart. Show me what is true about myself, and thank You for drawing me close to You today. Amen."

Adversity Teaches Us to Depend on God
DAY 3: HOW TO GET MORE FAITH

Faith is essential to the Christian life. We are saved through faith (Ephesians 2:8, 9), we live by faith (Habakkuk 2:4), and "without faith it is impossible to please God" (Hebrews 11:6).

But what is faith? Faith is that essence that gives reality and proof to things that are unseen, treating them as if they were already objects of sight rather than of hope. As George Mueller said, "It is time for faith to work when sight ceases." Faith is "belief in action."

In Luke 17:5 the disciples asked Jesus, "Increase our faith." Apparently, faith can grow.

What types of faith are described below?

1. Matthew 16:8 and 17:20

   How can God use this kind of faith?

Facing Adversity

2.   Matthew 15:28

What factors cause faith to actually increase?

3.   Romans 10:17

    a.   How do we get faith?

    b.   By implication, how might we get "more" faith?

4.   II Thessalonians 1:3, 4

    a.   What "size" of faith existed among the believers in Thessalonica?

    b.   According to verse 4, what circumstances had this church been enduring?

           Do you think that perhaps those circumstances may have spurred on their spiritual growth?

God has given to every believer a measure of faith (Romans 12:3) which is not static. What we do with the faith allotted to us has eternal consequences. It is during times of adversity that we are given great opportunity to see our faith grow.

Adversity often removes things in which we have put our trust. The Lord, in His mercy, places us in situations where we will only trust in Him. During trials our faith and hope in Him has an opportunity to rapidly grow.

Week 5: Adversity Teaches Us to Depend on God

God wants each of us to "grow up in all aspects into Him" (Ephesians 4:15), and to be thoroughly mature; firmly rooted, built up, and established in our faith (Colossians 1:7). Adversity is a key ingredient in this growth process.

Church history, as well as the lives of individuals throughout time, demonstrate the fact that trials and persecution can cause us to flourish and grow stronger. We see that "the tips of all adversity are dipped in divine love" for divine purposes; for the ultimate good of teaching us to depend on God Himself.

5. II Peter 1:5-8

    What does increasing faith and godliness prepare us for (before the Lord Jesus Christ?)

God will often remove those things in our lives that have "propped" us up so that we will have to depend solely on Him. In an effort to increase our faith, God may mercifully remove those things from our lives that hinder our ability to focus on Him. He may even remove "blessings" from our lives so that we will put our eyes back on the "Blesser" Himself.

Have you ever noted that your own faith has increased as you have endured difficult times? Describe that situation and how it impacted your life.

Have you asked the Lord to "increase your faith?" If not, ask Him now. And commit to Him that it is your heart's desire to cooperate with Him as He causes your faith to grow.

> ***"Oh Father, I want to trust You more; I need more faith. And since You use seasons of adversity to cause people's faith to grow, I'm asking You to use this trial to make my faith grow, too. Today I choose not to panic, not to run away, and not to become bitter over the difficulty that I face. I choose to trust You completely. Please don't let me waste this opportunity to grow spiritually. Increase my faith, Lord! Amen."***

Facing Adversity

Adversity Teaches Us to Depend on God

DAY 4: HOW TO STRENGTHEN MY FAITH

Faith is essential in the Christian life.

1. Romans 14:23

    If we do something without faith, what does God call it?

Yesterday, we saw how God uses trials in our lives to cause our faith to increase. Today we will see how the Lord often uses adversity to strengthen and enrich the faith that we already possess.

2. I Peter 1:3-7.

    a. What does Peter refer to as being more precious than gold?

    (The term "proof" found in verse 7 refers to "a test, trial, or criterion" used to determine a thing's adequacy.)

    b. Why is it more precious than gold?

    c. What have these believers been experiencing for awhile?

    (The word distressed here means "tension, pressure, or to be thrown off balance.")

Week 5: Adversity Teaches Us to Depend on God

    d.   What was this situation doing to their faith?

    e.   What does Peter remind them will be the result of this "testing by fire?"

    f.   What response does this elicit from those believers?

3.   Hebrews 11:1-40.

    a.   In this "hall of fame" how did these believers gain approval?

    b.   Is it possible to please God without faith?

           If we are doing "good" things, but don't have faith, can we please Him?

    c.   What kinds of adversity did these "men of old" face?

According to verse 39, what correlation, if any, do you see between the trials that they endured and the faith that they had?

Based on these verses, does demonstrating pure faith guarantee easy living or a comfortable resolution to life's problems?

Facing Adversity

"You are my Abba; my Daddy. And I know that You always want what is best for me. I know that as the heat is being turned up in my life through this trial, You are burning away the 'junk' in my life. Even though this time of testing is difficult, I know that You are using it to strengthen and purify my faith so that it will be like pure gold. Lord, that's what I really want! Give me the grace to welcome and not resist Your hand in my life today. Amen."

"Seven Times Hotter"
(Daniel 3:13-30)
(Judy Gerry)

The fire is seven times hotter than it's ever been before.
The flames explode with blasting winds that scream with death and roar.
The hearts of men around me melt as we draw near
These snapping violent flames. They fall dead in burning fear.

The fire is seven times hotter than most men will ever see,
This blurry-blue blaze is designed to destroy and uniquely consume me.
"Perhaps I'll die," I ponder as approaching the heat gets intense,
"But God can deliver and perhaps He will," for His power is immense.

The furnace is opened and there is no time to survey the situation,
No wading in slowly, no time to explore the options at fringe locations,
For I'm thrown in the middle, the hottest part,
as I'm shrouded in flames of death.
But I'm still alive! It's not even hot as I drink in long, cool breaths.

Once inside it looks so different, the threat and fear are gone.
And I guess I shouldn't be surprised that I am not alone.
Not only can God deliver me and protect from this infernal power,
He's right here with me, we are as one - this is my finest hour!

After the furnace flames flicker and the roaring blaze subdues
I come from the fiery pit stronger, and nothing did I lose
But those ropes that held me in bondage, a captive among men.
My Father vindicates me, and He gets the glory. Amen.

Week 5: Adversity Teaches Us to Depend on God

Adversity Teaches Us to Depend on God

DAY 5: PASSING THE TEST

The Old Testament prophet Daniel understood that until Christ's second coming, God's people would endure trials in order to "refine, purge, and make them pure" (Daniel 11:35).

We read those words and intellectually accept them as fact. We understand that the Lord intends to use adversity for our good. But somehow, trials seem to take us by surprise every time. Each trial of our life stands alone and every time that one intrudes into our lives we must decide how to respond.

What should be our attitude? Every individual has to grapple with this question. Today we will see how James, Peter and Paul responded when they encountered adversity.

1. James 1:2-4

    a. What kind of heart attitude does James say that we should have when we encounter various trials?

    b. Why should we have that specific attitude?

2. I Peter 1:6-8

    a. What kind of heart attitude does Peter say that we should have when we are distressed by various trials?

Facing Adversity

      b.   Why should we have that specific attitude?

3.   Romans 5:3-5

      a.   What kind of heart attitude does Paul say that we should have when we encounter tribulations?

      b.   Why should we have that specific attitude?

Do you believe that it really is possible to face adversity with joy? If so, what do you think is the key to having an attitude of rejoicing when times get hard?

When James tells us to "consider" it all joy, he is literally saying, "to judge, suppose or think, to lead the mind" a certain way. In other words, to "consider" adversity as joy means that we exert an act of our will, determined to see the facts in a certain way. Even though our minds may initially say otherwise, we are determined to believe that what God says is true.

Some may face adversity with a mindset to tough it out and begrudgingly endure the situation. But God calls us to "rejoice" and "exult" in our trials. When we are joyful we are outwardly demonstrating the inner truth of our faith in the Lord.

Rejoicing in the face of adversity is "faith in action."

Do you tend to respond to the various trials in your life with a heart of rejoicing?

Week 5: Adversity Teaches Us to Depend on God

Give a specific example of a time when you responded correctly:

Give an example of a time when you faced adversity but failed to respond correctly. What exactly would you do differently if you faced that same trial again in the future?

*"In the world you have tribulation, but take courage;
I have overcome the world."* (John 16:33)

"Lord, I admit that I don't always 'feel' joyful about this time of testing that I am facing. But You say that I should mentally choose to believe that You will use this adversity to accomplish something wonderful. So, I choose to believe You, Lord. Even though my feelings may lag behind, help me to place my confidence and joy on the truth of Your Word. Help me to pass this 'test' with true faith that grows stronger each day. Thank You, Lord. Amen."

Facing Adversity

WEEK 6

Adversity Clarifies our Purpose in Life

DAY 1: GOD HAS PLANS FOR ME

Our ultimate priority in life should be to seek God and to glorify Him. Even though Christians will usually give mental assent to this statement, their lives do not always reflect this priority.

Adversity will test what we are made of. It will reveal what is inside of us. Though our omniscient God already knows our response to trial, such bouts with suffering will aid and foster personal reevaluation of our hearts. Trials will help to clarify our purpose in life.

What do the following verses say about God's purpose for us?

1. Revelation 4:11

2. Ephesians 1:3, 4

Facing Adversity

3.   Colossians 1:21-23

4.   Romans 8:29

Summarize what you discern God's ultimate priority for you to be:

The Lord has *great plans* for each of our lives. We know He has goals regarding our eternal destiny, yet God's purpose and priority for us does not stop with salvation. He wants us to be sanctified, holy. What do the following verses say about daily life-goals?

5.   Matthew 6:33

   a.   What specific kinds of "things" is Jesus talking about "adding to us"?

   b.   In what ways are you seeking the kingdom of God on a daily basis?

   c.   Does the way that you spend your time reflect God's priorities?

6.   II Corinthians 5:9, 10

   a.   What motivated Paul to desire to please God?

   b.   Did the "fear of the Lord" (verse 11) affect the way that he lived?

Week 6: Adversity Clarifies our Purpose in Life

c. Do you have a deep desire to please God?

d. Is there anything that you are doing that you know does not please the Lord?

    A sin to give up?

    A habit to surrender?

e. Is there anything that you are not doing that you know would please Him?

    A kindness to perform?

    Some point of obedience?

"It is one thing to intellectually acknowledge that we know God's priority for our lives, and it's still another thing to say that we want to please God and experience His priorities for our lives. Yet, knowing and saying what is true does not comprise obedience. Obedience is faith in action. If we truly want to experience the Lord's plans for our lives we must put His priorities into action. We must follow through and 'DO IT!'"

"Lord, You created me for Your pleasure and Your great desire is for me to be completely holy. I want to please You, Lord. I want to know You intimately. But I confess that I get so easily distracted from pursuing You. Help me to take my thoughts captive and please guard my heart and mind in Christ Jesus so that I can experience Your plan for my life. That is what I truly yearn for. I love You, Lord. Amen."

Facing Adversity

Adversity Clarifies Our Purpose in Life

DAY 2: WANTING THE RIGHT THINGS

Its one thing to know what God wants for our lives; it's another thing to actually desire what God desires for us. We need to see what the Lord sees when He looks at us. We need to feel what He feels when He's near us. We need to share His heart and His point of view.

Note your insights regarding the following Scripture:

1. Psalm 73:25, 28

   Does David's statement match your heart's desire?

2. Philippians 3:7-10

   a. How did Paul view the things that he used to value?

   Recalling Paul's past history, did Paul initiate getting rid of those things, or did God forcibly strip him of these wrong priorities?

   b. Was it loving of God to do that to Paul?

   c. What did Paul gain by relinquishing those things that he had previously held onto with delight?

   d. Do you want to gain those same things?

Week 6: Adversity Clarifies our Purpose in Life

    e.   What do you have to do in order to gain them?

Has the Lord ever taken anything away from you that, in retrospect, you see had been taking His rightful "first place" in your life? Describe the situation:

    Did you consider that painful experience to be "adversity?"

    Did you initially "rejoice" at the opportunity to realign your priorities?
    Are you counting it all joy now?

    After God took it away, were you able to experience the nearness of God in a more fresh and vital way?

"Jesus, You are the Lover of my soul! Whenever I'm in Your presence I crave knowing You more and I never want to leave Your side. Those times are precious to me. I wish that I experienced that closeness with You all of the time, but my heart is prone to wander. Thank You for pursuing me, and for relentlessly scouring my heart of those 'loves' that seduce me away from You. Thank You for using the difficulties of my life to pull me into Your arms, because there is nowhere else that I would rather be! Amen."

Facing Adversity

Adversity Clarifies Our Purpose in Life
DAY 3: PURSUING THE RIGHT THINGS

We all know people who say one thing and do another. Many of us say that we desire what the Lord wants for our lives; yet, our actions say otherwise. The truth is that our actions reflect the real priorities of our hearts.

1. Matthew 7:24-27.

    a. Two men each built a house. What differentiated the construction of these two homes?

    b. What differences in adversity did each experience?

    c. What results did each experience?

Have you ever seen one person fall, and yet, another person stand strong, after they have endured identical adversity? If so, to what to you attribute the success of the victorious one?

Would you say that your life is typified by wisely building your time, energies, and assets on "rock?"

Do you need to rebuild some of your "sandy soil" efforts on bedrock? (even in the little things?)

Week 6: Adversity Clarifies our Purpose in Life

In Jesus' parable of the two homes built on the sandy soil and on the rock, Jesus pointed out that the difference between the two lay in whether or not the construction engineer "acted" upon God's words. Note what the following verses say about our actions.

2. II Peter 3:10

3. I Corinthians 3:13, 14

4. Luke 10:38-42

    a. What one thing is really necessary?

    b. Do your actions reflect this priority?

Adversity can be the catalyst that motivates us to pursue the right priorities. Note any insights from the following verses:

5. Psalm 119:67

6. Psalm 119:71

7. Psalm 107:20

Have you thanked God for mercifully intervening to help you establish correct priorities in your life? In your journal, write out a prayer of thanksgiving to Him right now.

Facing Adversity

*"Only the heart that is emptied of its own things
can receive the things of God."*
(Hannah Whitall Smith)

Adversity Clarifies Our Purpose in Life
DAY 4: LOOKING LIKE CHRIST

God's will for us is "that we should be holy and blameless before Him" (Ephesians 1:3, 4), and "conformed to the image of His Son" (Romans 8:29).

What does it mean to be in the "image" of Christ? We can try to act like Christ, and even successfully appear to be Christlike through imitation. But God wants more than imitation. It is His will that the life of Christ be actually lived through us.

"Self" competes with Christ for rulership in our lives. "Self" is that part of us, also called the "flesh," that wants its own way. It does not want to say to God, "not as I will, but as Thou wilt" (Matthew 26:39). "Self" says "this plan of mine is a good one, so please bless it, God." Rather than being available to be used in God's plan, "self" wants God to fit into its own plan.

What does the Lord say about "self" in the following verses?

1. Romans 12:1, 2

> In Hebrew culture, an animal sacrifice deemed valuable to the owner was placed on the altar to be killed. God viewed such offerings as being a spiritual service of worship.
>
> According to verse 2, what about "self" must become "transformed?"

Week 6: Adversity Clarifies our Purpose in Life

2. Ephesians 4:22-24

    a. What are we to do with the "old self?"

    b. How do we get the "new self?"

    c. According to verse 23, what about the "old self" needs to be "renewed?"

3. Romans 6:3-7

    What happens to the "old self?"

4. Galatians 2:20

    a. What has happened to the "old self"?

    b. Who is living the Christian life "in" us?

In order for the life of the indwelling Christ to live through us there must be the death of our "selves." Sins need to be confessed, but self must be crucified. God is not looking for "self-improvement" but for "self-crucifixion." And crucifixion feels painful – it feels like adversity.

Christlikeness is not an imitation of a life, but the impartation of a new life - His life.

Do you truly desire to be conformed to the image of Christ?

Facing Adversity

Can you recall a time when you placed yourself on the altar as your spiritual service of worship; yielding every part of your being to the Lord for His use? If not, why not do that today?

Have you ever tried to live the Christian life in the strength of your "old self" without the power of Christ? If so, what was the result?

> *"Heavenly Father, I need to have my mind transformed so that I can become like Jesus. As I've faced this trial that I'm going through, I've tried to 'look like' Christ, but I know deep down that I have many wrong thoughts and attitudes inside. Change me, Lord. My 'self' can't do it. I need You to change me from the inside out, and You've promised that You can and You will. I believe You, Lord. Thank You. Amen."*

Adversity Clarifies Our Purpose in Life
DAY 5: BEING LIKE CHRIST

We can be partakers of Christ's "divine nature" through faith in what only He can provide (II Peter 1:3, 4). The Christian's strength is in realizing the "mystery" that Christ lives in us (Colossians 1:26, 17). But even in Christians "self" keeps raising its ugly head and there is a struggle within us (Romans 7:22-24).

1. Galatians 5:17-25

    a. What opposes the Spirit of God who indwells us?

    b. What are the deeds of the flesh?

Week 6: Adversity Clarifies our Purpose in Life

    c.   What is the fruit of the Spirit?

    d.   If we belong to Christ what have we done?

In order to experience the victorious life of Christ in us, "self" must be crucified. Picture a person crucified on a cross much like Christ was crucified. Every slight movement is painful. All independence is gone as his limbs are restrained. He is totally helpless and must rely totally upon others. He is dying.

That is exactly where God wants us. He wants "our flesh, with all of its passions and desires," to be crucified (Galatians 5:19-21,24). He wants us to depend wholly upon Himself. Any area of life where we've not learned to be dependent, is an area of life where we've not yet repented. It is precisely in those areas that we must be crucified.

This experience is painful (Philippians 1:29). We don't want to give up our self-will and desires. But the result of dying to self enables Christ to truly live through you as you become totally dependent upon Him.

2.   Luke 9:23

    What does it mean to you to "crucify yourself?"

    ("Taking up the cross" means consciously dying to the world and living for Christ.)

Crucifixion of your "self" cannot be done alone, but it involves cooperation with Another. You can take up your own cross, but Someone else has to drive the nails, hoist up the cross, and plant it in the ground. That other person is the Lord. Will we cooperate when the pain is inflicted?

The Lord may choose to use another person to help "nail you down" to the cross. Is there any individual in your life who irritates you? Might God be using this person to help you "die to self?"

It has been said that the only problem with a "living sacrifice" (Romans 12:1) is that it keeps crawling off of the altar. How often must we present our bodies to Christ, how often must we be crucified?

Facing Adversity

3.   I Corinthians 15:31

Can you say that you desire to have your "self" crucified so that Christ can live through you?

Does anything scare you about yielding your entire self to the Lord? If so, what?

Is there anything in your life that you are reluctant to "put on the altar;" anything that you are refusing to give up?

How have you responded to His efforts in your life to crucify your "old self?" Did you cooperate with Him?

Take time now to ask the Lord to live His life through you.

> *"Jesus, You are the Lamb of God; sacrificed for me. You ask me to be crucified with You, and though I can't grasp all that this means, I do know that pain is part of this Calvary road. Lord, You understand the hurt that I feel as I face this trial in my life. I receive this painful experience and present it to You as an offering, a sacrifice of my 'self' on the altar. I give You my 'self' and ask that You will exchange my life for Yours. Fill me with Your Holy Spirit, and live Your life through me. Thank You, Lord. Amen."*

WEEK 7

Adversity Prepares Us for Blessing
DAY 1: ADVERSITY PREPARES ME TO BLESS OTHERS

Born in 1820, Fanny Crosby had a challenging life. When she was only six weeks old a doctor's careless error resulted in her permanent blindness, and her father died when she was a child.

Many might respond to those circumstances with self-pity, resentment, or bitterness. But Fanny trusted that the Lord had a good plan for her life. In her autobiography she wrote, "It seemed intended by the blessed Providence of God that I should be blind all my life, and I thank Him for the dispensation."

Fanny began to write poetry, and during her lifetime wrote over 9,000 hymns. Her ministry reached millions and still continues to touch the lives of believers around the world.

She welcomed the trial of her blindness as a gift from God, saying, "I could not have written thousands of hymns if I had been hindered by the distractions of seeing all the interesting and beautiful objects that would have been presented to my notice." Fanny recognized that her adversity gave her a platform from which she could bless others.

Facing Adversity

Adversity will either harden us or soften us. If we allow God to soften us through trials we will be pliable, prepared, and usable to God. The life of Paul bears witness that often it is the trial itself that opens the door of opportunity for ministry.

1. Acts 16:22-33

    a. What adversity did Paul and Silas face after they preached the gospel?

    b. How did the Lord use their adverse situation to further the gospel?

2. Acts 16:36-17:4

    a. How did the policemen's response in Philippi actually end up furthering Paul and Silas' ministry?

3. Acts 17:5-12

    a. What kind of adversity did Paul and Silas face in Thessalonica?

    b. How did that adversity expand their ministry?

4. Acts 7:13-15

    a. What kind of adversity did Paul and Silas face in Berea?

    b. How did that adverse situation further their missionary ministry?

Week 7: Adversity Prepares Us for Blessing

Had Paul encountered smooth sailing in the cities along the way, he may have not traveled as quickly to bring the word of Christ to the Gentile world. Paul's missionary ministry was propelled by the winds of adversity.

5. Philippians 1:12-14

    a. What specific trial was Paul enduring at this time?

    b. What ministry opportunity was opened to Paul as a direct result of these adverse circumstances?

Most of us would agree that being chased by mobs would qualify as adversity. We would lament the burden of blindness or physical beatings. We would likely refer to long-term false imprisonment as being a trial.

And yet, those very trials enabled Fanny, Paul, Silas, and others to have ministry opportunities that they would not have otherwise experienced.

Have you ever experienced a time of adversity that opened new doors of ministry in your own life?

Can you see how the Lord has used your personal pain to bring blessing to others?

If so, thank the Lord for using you, and for the ministry privilege that He has entrusted to you.

"Light of the World, illuminate this trial that I am facing and show me how You want to use it to open a door of ministry for me. I believe that You can change what seems like a 'setback' in my life to become a 'steppingstone' of blessing. Shine Your light on me so I can take joy in what You are doing, and help me to cooperate with Your intricately perfect plan. Amen."

Facing Adversity

Adversity Prepares Us for Blessing

DAY 2: ADVERSITY PREPARES ME TO COMFORT OTHERS

Those in pain yearn to be comforted.

The Lord Himself is our comforter. He says, "I, even I, am He who comforts you. As one whom his mother comforts, so I will comfort you" (Isaiah 51:12; 66:13).

The Lord cares so deeply about our suffering that He left us His Holy Spirit whom He calls "the Comforter" (John 16:7). He also left the church body to minister comfort to those who are in pain (II Corinthians 7:6, 7).

Our own adversity is a key element in preparing us to comfort others. The way that we respond to our own trials will determine whether or not God can use us to minister comfort to others during their seasons of pain. If we turn to the Lord for comfort rather than turning away from Him in anger, then He can teach us how to comfort others.

Before experiencing trials, we may think that we know the answers to the questions of suffering. We may have theories on how to comfort others before we ourselves have been comforted through the fires of testing. But there is nothing like a little experience to upset a theory.

Job was a man who endured monumental suffering. His friends meant well and tried to comfort him, but they misunderstood what was happening in Job's life.

As Job discovered, many people are prone to trivialize what the Lord is doing in another's life. We may insensitively refuse to acknowledge the depth of another's pain, or even brush away their misery by lightly saying, "Tomorrow will be better... just hang in there" (Job 17:10-12 paraphrase).

How do "those who are at ease" tend to respond to others' suffering?

1. Psalm 123:4

2. Job 12:5

Week 7: Adversity Prepares Us for Blessing

Still others may assume that suffering is a direct result of personal sin. Job was a righteous man, yet how did his friends "comfort" him?

3.   Job 18:20, 21; 22:21-23

Have you found that some people actually added to your personal pain during dark times in your life? If so, what have you found to be ineffective in encouraging others?

Edith Schaeffer says in her book *Affliction*:

> *"No one can really comfort anyone else unless there has been a measure of the same kind of affliction or some kind of suffering which has brought about an understanding and in which we have ourselves experienced the Lord's comfort."*

The Lord uses our pain to make us sensitive to others' situations. God used the suffering experienced by the Hebrews while captive in Egypt to tenderize them toward those who would become strangers in their own future country of Israel (Exodus 23:9). Nothing is wasted in God's economy. He will use our experiences in the valley of pain to accomplish something wonderful.

Job asked his friends, "How long will you torment me, and crush me with words?" (Job 19:1). Rather than hurting the wounded, we can learn how to encourage them as we ourselves are encouraged by the Lord.

4.   II Corinthians 1:3-6

What is one of the purposes for pain in a believer's life?

Facing Adversity

Have you seen in your own life that God uses you to comfort others in the same way that He, Himself, has comforted you?

What areas of pain are you most sensitive to in others?

Would you say that you have been hardened, or softened, by the adversity that you have experienced?

> *"Thank You for sending Your Holy Spirit to be my tender Comforter during the stormy days of my life. Thank You for always being with me. Help me to learn as I walk through these dark valleys. Lord, teach me to notice those who are in pain around me, and I ask that You will use me to comfort them in just the same way that You so faithfully comfort me. Your mercies really are new every morning. I love You, Lord. Amen."*

Adversity Prepares Us for Blessing
DAY 3: ADVERSITY TRAINS ME TO MEET TRUE NEEDS

Adversity trains us to discern and meet the true needs of those in pain.

The Lord specifically uses people to be His ambassadors of comfort to those who are in pain. Experiencing comfort through our own suffering can equip us to be the friend that other hurting people need.

Since those who are in pain tend to feel isolated and abandoned (Job 19:13,14), they need true friendship. Hurting people need others with whom they can be honest, without adding the pain of condemnation (Job 19:22). Job's friends rallied around him,

Week 7: Adversity Prepares Us for Blessing

encouraging him to discuss his suffering. Yet, when he was honest about his pain they reprimanded him (Job 15:1-6).

What can we give to friends who are enduring a time of pain? During your own times of trial, have you found other believers to be effective ministers of mercy to you? If so, what were the qualities of those who truly comforted you?

What does someone who is hurting really need?

1. Job 2:11-13

2. Job 6:14

3. Job 19:21

4. Proverbs 17:17

5. Romans 12:15

6. Job 19:25-27

    What was Job's greatest consolation?

The school of adversity can also be a training ground for developing discernment. As God uses the heat of affliction to mold us into the image of Christ, He gives us a different perspective on His divine design of adversity. As we watch others going through trials, we need to seek the Lord's direction as to how He would like us to respond in comforting them.

Facing Adversity

Comforting often means taking action.

7.   Luke 10:30-37

   a.   What did the Samaritan "feel?" (Verse 33)

   b.   What did the Samaritan "do?" (Verses 34, 35)

   c.   How did Jesus advise us to respond to similar situations? (Verse 37)

Comforting may also mean restraining from action.

8.   Luke 15:12-16.

   a.   What was the apparent need? (Verse 14)

   b.   Did anyone "do" anything for him? (Verse 16)

We later read that as a result of his hunger, the wayward son returned home to his father in repentance. If someone had intervened and fed this son while he remained in his sin, God's purposes for the adversity may have been short circuited.

"Empathy" is "your pain in my heart." While we may feel the pain of others, we must respond to that pain according to the Lord's will. Henry Blackaby says, "'Don't just stand there, DO something,' is often poor advice. The best advice may sometimes be, 'Don't just DO something, stand there!'"

We must seek the Lord's heart, and ask for discernment in order to meet the "true needs" of a person rather than merely the "perceived needs." It is imperative that we prayerfully not interfere with the lesson of suffering in another believer's life.

Week 7: Adversity Prepares Us for Blessing

9. Matthew 16:21-23

How did Peter wrongly try to offer pity and sympathy to Christ?

While Jesus refused the sympathy of men, He did accept the comfort of the Father and of angels (Luke 22:42, 43). We should always encourage the hurting to seek the comfort of the Lord.

We can be confident that the trials in our lives can be used by the Lord as a ministry of blessing to others. The comfort that we receive from the Lord makes us useful to Him in comforting those who are suffering and in meeting their deepest needs.

Like everything in the Christian life, we must receive guidance from the Holy Spirit as to how to specifically minister to the hurts of others. We need to seek His heart and hear His voice:

> *"The Lord God has given Me the tongue of disciples, that I may know how to sustain the weary one with a word. He awakens Me morning by morning. He awakens My ear to listen as a disciple." (Isaiah 50:4)*

"Jesus, thank You for sending people into my life to comfort me during my times of deep pain. What a blessing they are to me. Like them, I want to be able to help others who are hurting, but sometimes I don't know what people really need. Forgive me for jumping in and trying to ease other's pain without first talking with You about it. Please give me Your wisdom and discernment so that I can comfort people in ways that lead them, and me, to seek Your face. Amen."

Facing Adversity

"Encouragement"
(Judy Gerry)

Oh please don't say it's easy, for the pain is often deep,
And to say the trial is nothing makes deliverance look cheap.

To say that winter soon will pass and clouds will go away
May not be true. Please cheer me on to trust God and obey.

Acknowledge, but don't wallow in my pain to whine and wail,
For in my weakness Christ is strong and faithfully prevails.

Encourage me, and help me keep a godly, balanced view,
That pain is real, but God transcends all that I'm going through.

Adversity Prepares Us for Blessing
DAY 4: ADVERSITY PREPARES ME TO RECEIVE BLESSING TODAY

For the past few days we have seen how our seasons of adversity prepare us for blessing others. Trials can actually open doors of ministry for us; they teach us how to comfort others when they are hurting and adversity trains us to recognize and meet others' true needs.

Adversity not only leads us to BECOME a blessing to others; trials prepare us to RECEIVE personal blessing from God.

The Lord tells us in I Peter 3:9 that when we are abused by others we are to give them a blessing. Why? "For you were called for the very purpose that you might inherit a blessing."

In other words, when we are willing to suffer righteously without retaliation, we have a wonderful opportunity to experience and inherit blessing from the Lord. This reward from the Lord is not only to be experienced in the future; it is experienced in the here-and-now.

Week 7: Adversity Prepares Us for Blessing

Look up the verses below and record any personal blessing that results from suffering righteously.

1. II Corinthians 1:5

2. II Corinthians 4:8-10

3. II Timothy 1:8, 12

4. Daniel 3:13-25

5. Psalm 81:7

6. I Peter 4:14

7. Philippians 3:8

In light of the place in life where you are today, which of the above verses encourages you the most?

As you consider the painful episodes of your life, can you see how God has used those experiences to bless you?

Facing Adversity

"O Lord, I love it here in the furnace because You are here. I love the unique intimacy that we share when You speak to me during the tempest. I love knowing that You are completing the work that You have started in my life. I love knowing that even if I lose everything; I win You. O, I love You! Thank You for bringing me to this place where I can experience the joy of knowing You in ways I never could have without this storm. Amen."

Adversity Prepares Us for Blessing

DAY 5: ADVERSITY QUALIFIES ME TO RECEIVE FUTURE BLESSING

When we encounter adversity and respond in a biblical way, there is great reward and blessing for us. When we share in Christ's sufferings, He meets our needs and we also share in His glory. What a joy that we can experience the presence, power, and comfort of the Lord in our daily lives.

When we trust the Lord during the "momentary affliction" of our lives, He rewards us with great eternal blessings. Look up the following verses and fill in the chart.

Scripture	Facts About Suffering	The Resulting Blessing
Philippians 2:8,9		
1 Peter 5:10		
Matthew 5:11,12		

Week 7: Adversity Prepares Us for Blessing

Scripture	Facts About Suffering	The Resulting Blessing
Romans 8:17,18		
2 Corinthians 4:16-18		
Hebrews 10:32-34		
Hebrews 13:12-14		
1 Peter 4:12-14		
James 1:12		
Matthew 19:27-30		
2 Timothy 2:12		

Facing Adversity

When we walk through valleys of suffering, our true reward is found in pleasing the Lord. Any other reward that we may receive is simply a by-product of our relationship with Jesus.

What a privilege it is to know Him (Philippians 3:8) and to anticipate an eternity by His side (Revelation 22:3, 4). Hallelujah!

"Lord, I get so wrapped up in the here and now. I need a glimpse of eternity; my life is so short, and eternity is long. The loss and pain that I experience today is brief compared to the lavish reward that is coming. Don't let me grow weary of doing well; help me to remember what You have promised to me as I run this race called 'life.' I can hardly wait to see You at the finish line. Come quickly, Lord Jesus! Amen."

WEEK 8

Adversity Is an Invitation from God
DAY 1: MAKING THE CHOICE

As children of God we can be confident that any adversity allowed to enter our lives is an *invitation from God* to join Him as he makes us more like Jesus. How we respond to that invitation demonstrates our current relationship with the Lord and reveals much about our future.

This invitation requires an R.S.V.P. The way that we respond to trials and duress determines whether we become bitter, or better.

We have a choice to make. And making that choice is a spiritual battle.

Battles or struggles in our lives may appear to be "routine" events of mundane life. However, Paul reminds us that we are in a spiritual battle (Ephesians 6:10-12).

The battle for spiritual growth is raging in our lives, and it is won or lost in the seemingly "minor skirmishes" of our attitude and perspective. The battlefield begins in our minds. "As a man thinks within himself, so is he" (Proverbs 23:7).

Victory and spiritual growth is secured when we "have this attitude in yourselves which was also in Christ Jesus" (Philippians 2:5). Paul maintains that "we have the mind of Christ" (I Corinthians 2:16).

Facing Adversity

When we do not respond properly to the adversity which the Lord allows into our lives, we are not experiencing the "mind of Christ." If we are unaware of the battle being waged for our thoughts and attitudes, we are easy prey for the evil one and his minions.

1. II Corinthians 10:3-5

    a. What are we to destroy?

    b. What are we to take captive?

2. Philippians 4:8

    a. What eight things are we to think about?

    _____ _____ _____ _____

    _____ _____ _____ _____

We are literally to "frisk" every thought that seeks entry into our minds. Every thought that we entertain must meet the criterion of Philippians 4:8. Any thought that fails the test must be captured and sent away.

Are we willing to see our lives from God's point of view and cooperate with Him? Or will we insist on defending ourselves, rejecting His invitation to join Him as He makes us more like Jesus?

Our initial tendency to blame others, to become angry, or to indulge in self pity must be vehemently resisted (Ephesians 4:26-32; I Peter 2:23). We must harness our thoughts and remember what is true:

Week 8: Adversity Is an Invitation from God

- Nothing can enter our life without God's permission.
- God is in total control.
- He loves us, and
- Everything that He does is for our good.

God assures us that He will not allow us to be tempted above what we're able to endure (I Corinthians 10:13). He promises that He'll always give us sufficient grace to persevere (II Corinthians 12:9).

3. Hebrews 12:15

   a. What will limit the work of God's grace in our lives?

   b. Allowing such a "root" to spring up in our lives will cause trouble. How will it affect those around us?

   c. Who are the people around you who might be affected by your allowing such a "root" to spring up?

If we face adversity with bitterness we will always lose the battle. We must also remember what is at stake if we choose bitterness.

4. Ruth 1:19-21

   a. How did Naomi respond to her adversity?

   b. Whose reputation(s) were slandered because of her bad attitude?

5. Numbers 14:26-33

Facing Adversity

a. How did the Israelites respond to their trials in the desert?

b. Who would suffer because of their attitudes?

Remember, choosing bitterness will always take us where we don't want to go:

- It poisons and defiles the people around us (Hebrews 12:15).

- It harms our testimony and slanders God's reputation as being kind (Ruth 1:19-21)

- It guarantees another round of adversity (Numbers 14:26-33).

As you consider a trial that is in your life today, ask yourself the following questions:

 Am I willing to work to take my thoughts captive?

 Will I refuse to entertain thoughts and attitudes that are not true from God's perspective?

 Am I willing to completely forgive others and reject any bitterness that is taking root in my soul?

 Am I willing to humble myself and receive this adversity as God's personal invitation for good in my life?

The Lord awaits your answer. What choice do you make?

"My gracious Father, it is sobering to realize that my adversity is really a personal invitation from You for me to grow spiritually. I confess that I have harbored bitter thoughts and blamed others for my pain. I recognize that there is a battle raging for my mind; a spiritual battle. Lord, from this point on I choose to reject bitterness by taking my thoughts captive so that I can obey You. It is a choice, and I choose to cooperate with Your work in my life. By faith, I accept Your invitation. Thank You, Lord. Amen."

Week 8: Adversity Is an Invitation from God

Adversity Is an Invitation from God
DAY 2: ACCEPTING GOD'S INVITATION TO REPENT

Yesterday we learned that any adversity allowed to enter our lives is an *invitation from God* to join Him as he makes us more like Jesus. This invitation requires an R.S.V.P.

Let's look at R.S.V.P. as an acronym for our response to His call. Today we begin with the first step in our response; R - REPENTANCE

In Week 4 we saw how adversity is often the result of our personal sin. Trials can bring to light areas of disobedience and pride that we may need to confess. When the Lord allows adversity into our lives it is often His merciful invitation for us to quickly repent (Lamentations 3:39-41).

Spend some time today reviewing your responses to the questions in Week 4. Consider a trial that you are currently facing. Might the adversity that you are experiencing be, in some way, the result of your sin?

1. Psalm 139:23, 24

    a. If the Lord reveals to you that there is some unconfessed sin in your life, immediately assume personal responsibility for that sin. Rather than blaming others, ask the Lord to show you where you have been wrong in your actions or attitudes. Write your thoughts below.

    b. Ask the Lord to help you discover the weakness through which that sin crept into your life. Write your prayer below.

    c. Acknowledge that God wants to use your current painful situation to accomplish good in your life. Praise Him for it.

Facing Adversity

2. Joel 2:13

How does the Lord respond when we repent from our sin?

Repentance can change our circumstances and often result in lessened adversity (II Chronicles 12:6-12). Yet our greatest reward is that we experience the joyful fellowship of the Lord in a fresh and revived way.

Spend some time today thanking the Lord for how He loves you so much that He won't let you "get away with your sin."

"My Redeemer, thank You for purchasing eternal forgiveness for every sin that I'll ever commit. You have been showing me areas where I've allowed sin to creep into my heart and life. These sins have been slowly gnawing away at my soul and separating me from You. I can see how my trials have often been the direct result of these sins. I am guilty, Lord, and I am sorry. I commit today to totally turn away from those sins and completely turn toward You. I want to be wholly Yours. I love you, Lord. Amen."

Adversity Prepares Us for Blessing
DAY 3: EMBRACING THE OPPORTUNITY TO GROW

For many weeks we have examined how the Lord wants to use adversity in our lives to carry us into seasons of blessing. Any adversity that He allows to enter our lives is an "invitation" from Him that requires an R.S.V.P.

Yesterday we dealt with the R – REPENTANCE. We were reminded that some adversity is the direct result of our sin, and were exhorted to repent of any unconfessed sin in our lives.

Week 8: Adversity Is an Invitation from God

Once we are confident that there is no unconfessed sin in our lives, we know that our pain has come from either Satan or God. The Lord God controls everything that enters our lives, so even when pain is inflicted by the evil one, it is only there by permission of God our Father (Job 1:12; II Corinthians 12:7).

That brings us to the next letter in our response to the Lord: S – SURRENDER. We should respond to all adversity with a heart that totally desires God's will; even if it requires our suffering. We need to surrender our plans, our future, and our comfort to the God who loves us.

1. Acts 5:40, 41

    Why were the apostles rejoicing that they had suffered?

We all would love to respond to our trials as those apostles responded. What specific steps might we take to help ensure our godly response when we see the storms heading our way? Look up the following verses and fill in the blanks below:

   a. Romans 8:16, 17
   When unexpected pain strikes the first thing that we should do is reaffirm that we are _____ of God.

   b. II Corinthians 12:9 and Hebrews 4:15, 16

   As His children we can cling to the promises of God's sustaining and abundant _____ to meet our needs.

   c. II Corinthians 12:7

   We can ask the Lord to show us the _____ that He is allowing this pain to enter our life.

   d. II Corinthians 12:8; Matthew 26:39 and II Chronicles 20:6-12

   We can ask God to _____ the painful trial.

Facing Adversity

2.   I Thessalonians 5:18

        a.   For what should we be thankful?

        b.   Why should we be thankful?

Spend some time today reviewing your responses to the questions from Weeks 5 and 6. As you consider the trial that you are now facing, thank the Lord for giving you this opportunity to grow spiritually. Thank Him for the way He is "conforming you to the image of Christ" (Romans 8:29).

Remember, no normal person chooses to suffer; but a healthy believer will always choose God's will even if it means suffering.

"How easy it would be to say, 'Thy will be done,' if we could once recognize that trouble meant only and always blessing for us."
(Hanna Whitall Smith)

"How wonderful that I can call you 'Abba'; for You are my loving Father and I am Your little child! I believe Your promises that everything You're allowing into my life is being used to help me grow up to become mature as Your child. Father, don't stop what You're doing; keep teaching me and training me. My great desire is to be counted worthy as Your child. It is such a privilege to belong to You, and when I grow up I want to be just like You. Thank You, Abba. Amen."

Week 8: Adversity Is an Invitation from God

Adversity Prepares Us for Blessing

DAY 4: KEEP HANGING IN THERE

Some trials are quickly resolved in our lives, but when adversity continues for a long time the child of God can become weary. How do we keep going when the race that we are running is more of a *marathon* than a *sprint*?

How do we hang in there so that we can cross the finish line in victory?

Adversity in our lives is "God's invitation" to cooperate with His plan for our lives. As we experience R – REPENTANCE and then S – SURRENDER our will to Him, we will experience V – VICTORY in our lives.

Victory is won when we are able to "run with endurance the race set before us" so that we can run into Jesus' arms at the finish line (Hebrews 12:1).

In order to persevere we must continually remind ourselves of what is true as discussed this week on Day 1. We must thoughtfully cultivate a deep trust in the sovereignty of God.

1. Genesis 50:20

    Can you see how God might use your current circumstances for good?

It is also helpful to familiarize ourselves with the biblical accounts of how God's servants dealt with adversity. What an encouragement their lives are! We can learn much from their successes and failures as we faithfully bathe our minds in God's Word.

With which character in the Bible do you most readily identify?

Did that person face any trial or pain in life? How did they respond?

Facing Adversity

Can you think of specific individuals in the Bible who faced adversity similar to what you are facing? How did they respond?

In Week 7 we saw how God can use our adversity to present us with a platform for ministry. When you become weary through a long season of trials, take time to meditate on specific ways that the Lord can use your experience to minister to others.

Most importantly, commit yourself to consistently focus on what is eternal. That is the focal point of our hope (Titus 2:13)! Your commitment to faithfully endure trials will result in great reward. There is a lot at stake if you will hang in there.

Look up the following verses and write them out word for word. Don't be tempted to skip this exercise; it will feed your soul (Matthew 4:4)!

1. Write out Colossians 3:2-4

2. Write out Philippians 3:13, 14

3. Write out II Corinthians 5:9, 10

4. Write out James 1:12

In the space below, summarize the message of the four texts above:

Week 8: Adversity Is an Invitation from God

Are they an encouragement to you?

"One ship drives east and another west with the self-same winds that blow: It's the set of the sail, not the strength of the gale that determines the way we go." (Ella Wheeler Wilcox, "Winds of Fate")

"Lord, on days when I feel discouraged remind me of what is true. Remind me that You're waiting for me at the finish line of this 'race' called 'life.' Remind me that You are cheering me on as I run through the difficult valleys, and that You have given me everything that I need for victory. Remind me of what is at stake in how I run, and help me to persevere. Lord, compel me to keep my eyes on You, for You are my true reward. Maranatha!"

Adversity Prepares Us for Blessing
DAY 5: EMBRACE ADVERSITY WITH JOY

We are not random beings in the universe. We are God's special creation; His treasured ones (Psalm 83:3). We're His very own children whom He loves (John 1:12).

He has a plan for us determined before we were even born (Jeremiah 29:11; Psalm 139:16). We are not *pawns in the game of life*; we are co-heirs with the living Son of God (Romans 8:17). He is intimately involved with every detail concerning us (Psalm 139:16), and He intentionally uses adversity in our lives for our good and for His glory.

When trials come knocking at our door we can be assured that it is a direct invitation from the Lord Himself. He is inviting us to join Him in accomplishing His plan for our life.

1. Job 23:10

    What does the Lord want to accomplish in us through our trials?

Facing Adversity

The mineral pyrite is known as "fool's gold." When gold is mined, pyrite is often mingled with the "real gold." In order to separate the "foolish" from the "real thing" the minerals must be subjected to heat. The purest gold must be refined in the crucible of fire.

The goldsmith heats the mineral to a precise temperature, taking care not to burn the precious metal. Then as impurities rise to the surface the dross is skimmed away. Ultimately, the goldsmith can peer into the pure liquid gold and see his own reflection.

Scripture says, "Now we see in a mirror dimly, but then face to face" (I Corinthians 13:12).

2. II Corinthians 3:18

    a. What reflection should we ultimately see when we look into *our mirror*?

    b. Are you willing to cooperate with the Lord as He accomplishes this in your life?

We have choices to make. Do we want our lives to be mingled with "fool's gold" or do we want to be the "real thing?"

Will we respond to adversity with the mind of Christ, or will we react unwisely to the inevitable trials of life?

> *"Please let me come out of this closer to You, more mature as Your child, with a skimming off of some of the impurities which are spoiling the reflection of Your face as You look at me."* (Edith Schaeffer)

To be entrusted with suffering can be seen as an honor and privilege. In a very real sense, adversity is a compliment from the Lord Himself.

God allowed Job to experience pain because He had confidence that Job would trust in Him through the most difficult trials of life (Job 1:8).

Week 8: Adversity Is an Invitation from God

When the apostles were beaten and imprisoned they rejoiced because "they had been considered worthy" to suffer for Christ's name (Acts 5:41).

What an honor to be entrusted with the reputation of God Almighty! Have you thanked the Lord for the great privilege He has given you to be entrusted with your particular suffering?

Over the past weeks we have walked with the Lord through our personal seasons of trial. As you consider what you have learned, what specific truth has most impacted your heart and mind?

How will your understanding of God's truth change the way that you respond to future trials? In other words, when the storm clouds gather around you next time, what will you do differently?

How would you counsel a non-believer who may be facing adversity?

How would you counsel a believer who is facing adversity?

We have choices to make. Will we obey what we know God says is true, even when it is difficult?

Joyfully embracing the storms of life "is not too difficult for you, nor is it out of reach" (Deuteronomy 30:11). God sets before us "the blessing and the curse. So choose life in order that you may live, you and your descendants, by loving the Lord your God, by obeying His voice, and by holding fast to Him" (Deuteronomy 30:19, 20).

Hold fast to the Lord during the tempests of life. Don't grow weary of trusting and obeying Him (Galatians 6:9). Hope in Him (Psalm 33:18). And though the winds may seem to howl too long, "be patient; strengthen your hearts, for the coming of the Lord is at hand" (James 5:8).

Facing Adversity

Look closely into the darkness and you will see Jesus standing beside you through the blackest night (Joshua 5:13-15).

Listen well during the most turbulent, dark, times. The Lord hears those who cry out to Him in the storm, and He answers. It is only during storms that we discover God hiding in the thunder (Psalm 81:7).

The Lord uniquely reveals Himself to us in the storm; inside the furnace (Daniel 3:25); in the whirlwind (II Kings 2:1, 11); in the lion's den and the fish's stomach (Daniel 6:22; Jonah 2:1). Wherever adversity takes you, God invites you to meet Him there.

The sweetest part of R.S.V.P.-ing is that once we accept the Lord's invitation, we have the breathtaking privilege of intimately experiencing His P – PRESENCE. And anytime that we are in God's presence there is fullness of joy (Psalm 16:11).

The invitations have been sent.

Will you join Him in His work?

Will you walk with Him through the storm?

Will you respond to His beckoning to become like Jesus?

Will you joyfully accept His invitation to enter into His presence?

"Lord, I accept! I accept the challenges and difficulties of my life as invitation from You. Thank You for loving me so much that You are using the adversities in my life to pursue me and pull me into Your arms. You have promised that good will result from this difficult time, and You have said that through this I will become like gold – what an honor and joy! So I R.S.V.P. today, and run through the darkness of this storm into the sunshine of Your presence with joy and thanksgiving. Amen and Hallelujah!"

Week 8: Adversity Is an Invitation from God

"The Whirlwind"
(Judy Gerry)

It had stormed for quite a long time and I tired of dreary days.
Knives of lightning slashed their death lines as I searched for sunny rays.
And the thunder roared behind me in pursuit from its black shroud.
I had hoped we'd soon be freed from those days of darkening clouds.

So I grabbed a rope and held fast asking God to give me power
Not to tremble at the strong blast or from lightning stabs to cower.
I held on and clenched my life-line and for storms to cease I prayed.
(It had stormed for quite a long time and I tired of dreary days.)

But the storm was just beginning. We were swallowed in the roar,
And then sucked inside, were spinning, in the turbulent black core.
Yes, the whirlwind had consumed us with no rope on which to cling,
We were slammed inside its death crush, then we sensed an awesome thing:

True, this storm is terrifying, but God made it just for me.
And with His will verifying it's the Lord, Himself, I see!
Through the roar His voice speaks solely and He tells me of His might.
I'm enveloped by Him wholly, resting calmly in His light.

This may be the wind to carry me to be at home with You,
Or perhaps it's temporary; let me see it from Your view.
But when storms endure a long time and I tire of dreary days,
Lord, I want to welcome whirlwinds as I seek Your hidden ways.

(II Kings 2:1,11; Job 37:9, 38:1, 40:6; Jeremiah 23:19, 30:23; Ezekiel 1:4)

Facing Adversity

SUGGESTED READING

Arthur, Kay. Lord, *Where Are You When Bad Things Happen?*, Portland, OR: Multnomah Press, 1992.

Billheimer, Paul E., *Don't Waste Your Sorrows*. Washington, PA: Christian Literature Crusade, 1977.

Christenson, Evelyn, *Gaining through Losing*, Wheaton, IL, Victor Books, 1980.

DeMoss, Nancy Leigh (co-authored with Tim Grissom), *Seeking Him,* Chicago, IL, Moody Publishers, 2004.

Edman, Dr. V. Raymond, *In Quiet and Confidence,* Wheaton Bible College.

Edwards, Gene, *A Tale of Three Kings.* Auburn MA, The SeedSowers, 1980.

Elliot, Elisabeth, *A Path Through Suffering*. Ann Arbor, MI: Servant Publications, 1990.

Fehsenfeld, Del Jr., *Joy in the Morning*. Life Action Ministries Calendar, 1990.

Fenelon, Francois de, *The Seeking Heart.* Auburn, MA, The SeedSowers. Volume 4, Library of Spiritual Classics.

Gothard, Bill, *Understanding the Winds of Adversity*. Institute in Basic Youth Conflicts, Supplementary Alumni Book Volume 7, 1981.

Hession, Roy, *When I Saw Him,* Where Revival Begins. Fort Washington, PA, Christian Literature Crusade, 1975.

Lewis, C.S., *The Problem with Pain*. Grand Rapids, MI, Zondervan, 2001.

Martin, James, *Suffering Man, Loving God*. San Francisco, CA: Harper and Row, 1990.

McGee, J. Vernon, *Why Do God's Children Suffer?,* Pasadena, CA, Thru the Bible Books, 1974.

Schaeffer, Edith, *Affliction*. Grand Rapids, MI, Baker Books, 1993.

Tada, Joni Eareckson and Steven Estes, *When God Weeps*. Grand Rapids, MI, Zondervan, 1997.

About the Author

Judy Gerry met the Lord Jesus Christ as her Savior when she was a young child. During her college years at the University of California at Riverside, Judy received training through the ministry of Campus Crusade for Christ. She attended their Institute of Biblical Studies where she received in-depth Bible training from some of the nation's top seminary professors. Those classes piqued her hunger for the Word of God.

In 1969 she graduated and joined the staff of Campus Crusade for Christ. She married Dave Gerry in 1971. By 1979, their lives were bustling as the parents of five youngsters. Realizing that children are a blessing from God, Dave and Judy relished the opportunity to love and train their children. Judy's greatest desire has always been to please the Lord by being a godly wife and mother. Today, all of their grown children are believers, and Judy and Dave agree that, "I have no greater joy than this, to hear of my children walking in the truth" (III John 4).

Judy and Dave have served together with Gideons Int., on the board of directors of Child Evangelism Fellowship in Denver, Colorado, in the 1980s, and were enthusiastic AWANA directors for many years. Judy continues to be active in her local "Moms-in-Touch" prayer group and mentoring "Mothers of Preschoolers."

She has been teaching and writing Bible studies for over thirty years. Her great delight is seeing believers experience the blessings of intimacy with the Lord, and victory in their lives, as they obediently follow God's "ancient paths" (Jeremiah 6:16).

Judy and Dave are enjoying their empty-nest years in Camarillo, California, as they mentor young families in their church, teach Bible studies, speak at retreats, delight in their grandchildren, and daily anticipate the return of the Lord Jesus Christ.

Ancient Paths Ministries

Ancient Paths Ministries is committed to redirecting contemporary culture back to the timeless truths of God's Word.

With an emphasis on the practical application of Scripture to everyday living, Dave and Judy Gerry provide Bible studies and resources for spiritual growth and maturity. As authors, Bible teachers, and conference speakers, they exhort others to pursue Jesus Christ and to know Him. It is through nurturing that relationship that one will discover the foundation of all issues of life. In addition to speaking at men's and women's conferences, Dave and Judy lead challenging weekend marriage retreats on, "How to Have an Intentional Marriage."

For more information contact:

Dave and Judy Gerry
P.O. Box 498
Somis, CA 93066
(805) 484-2808

E-mail: Judy@AncientPathsMinsitries.com
www.AncientPathsMinistries.com

LifeSong Publishers

Books for Everyone in Your Family

God... Should I Be Baptized?
ISBN 9780971830615
$10.99 96pp 8.5x11
For children 8-12

The Lord's Supper...Let's Get Ready!
ISBN 9780971830660
$10.99 96pp 8.5x11
For children 8-14

God's Plan... My Response
ISBN 9780971830608
$9.99 96pp 6x9
For Jr. Hi/ Hi School

Loving God's Word
by Seth Kniep
ISBN 9780971830684
15.99 (Softcover) 288pp 6x9
ISBN 9780971830691
20.99 (Hardcover) 288pp 6x9

Hope When the River Rages
by Nancy Kaltenberger
ISBN 9780971830677
12.99 192pp 5x8

Promises From the Olive Tree:
A Book of Hope, Instruction and
Encouragement for Parents
by Noreen Jacks
ISBN 9780979911606

Other Bible Studies by Judy Gerry

Ancient Paths for Modern Women Series

"This is what the Lord says: 'Stand at the crossroads and look; ask for the ancient paths, ask where the good way is, and walk in it, and you will find rest for your souls.'" (Jeremiah 6:16)

Walking With the Lord
ISBN 9780971830622
$11.99 100pp 7.5x10

Walking as Wives
ISBN 9780971830639
$11.99 112pp 7.5x10

Walking as Mothers and Homemakers
ISBN 9780971830646
$11.99 110pp 7.5x10

Walking in the Church and in the World
ISBN 9780971830653
$11.99 130pp 7.5x10

"Judy Gerry has dug deeply into the sacred records of the Bible to surface divine guidance for women in every generation. Here is a timely, reassuring and professionally crafted study resource which belongs in every church library and on the study agenda for thinking women..."

Howard G. Hendricks, Distinguished Professor, Dallas Theological Seminary

Contact: LifeSong Publishers
P.O. Box 183, Somis, CA 93066-0183
www.LifeSongPublishers.com
Toll-free: 866-266-6917
or your favorite bookstore